LEARN-TO-WRITE KOREAN

- Trace and write the proper stroke order.
- Identify names and sounds of the letters.

MIGHTYFORTRESS
PRESS

For free Korean tutorial videos, please visit:

www.mightyfortresspress.com

ISBN NO: 978-1-7328644-4-3
Text and illustrations Copyright 2021 by Mighty Fortress Press.

All rights reserved. Published by Mighty Fortress Press. No part of this book may be reproduced, stored in a retrieval system or transmitted in any form or by any means, electronic, mechanical, photocopying, recording, scanning or otherwise, except as permitted under Sections 107 or 108 of the 1976 United States Copyright Act, without the prior written permission of the Publisher. Requests to the Publisher for permission should be addressed to the Permissions Department, Mighty Fortress Press, 18411 Crenshaw Blvd. Suite 418 Torrance, CA 90504.

For general information on our other products, please contact our Customer Care Department within the U.S. by going to our website at www.mightyfortresspress.com.

Kang, Eunice, author.
Koh, Young Jae, book designer.
"Magic Hangul Collection"

This book belongs to :

이름:

Name:

내 이름은 _____ 입니다.

Nae ee-rum eun _____ eem-ni-da.
My name is _____ .

저는 ____ 살 입니다.

Juh-nun ____ sal eem-ni-da.
I am ____ years old.

NOTE TO PARENTS

Welcome to *Learn-To-Write Korean*! This book includes step-by-step directions on how to write the Korean alphabet. Each letter comes with a pronunciation guide of the name and the sound it makes; it also comes with a simple word with illustration. There are also practice sheets for tracing and handwriting the letters.

In the Korean language, every letter has a certain order in which it must be written. You can think of stroke order like having to follow a recipe by adding ingredients in the right order. If you go out of order, you might end up with a flop! Doing the proper stroke order is important to create beautiful Korean letters, syllables, and words. As a general rule, you write a letter with strokes from left to right and top to bottom. Similar to English, you combine Korean consonants and vowels to form syllables.

My Korean Alphabet Learn-To-Write Activity Book covers the following:
- 14 basic consonants
- 5 double consonants
- 10 basic vowels
- 11 double vowels
- 7 main/basic syllables

Thank you again for choosing this book and allowing me to present Korean as a second language to you and your family in a fun way.

Happy writing!

Sincerely,
Eunice Kang, Ph.D.

TABLE OF CONTENTS

Unit 1. Consonants (자음)

Unit 2. Double Consonants (쌍자음)

Unit 3. Vowels (모음)

Unit 4. Double Vowels (쌍모음)

Unit 5. Syllables (음절)

UNIT 1

자음
Consonants

Note: In this unit, we will learn how to write the 14 basic consonants.

ㄱ

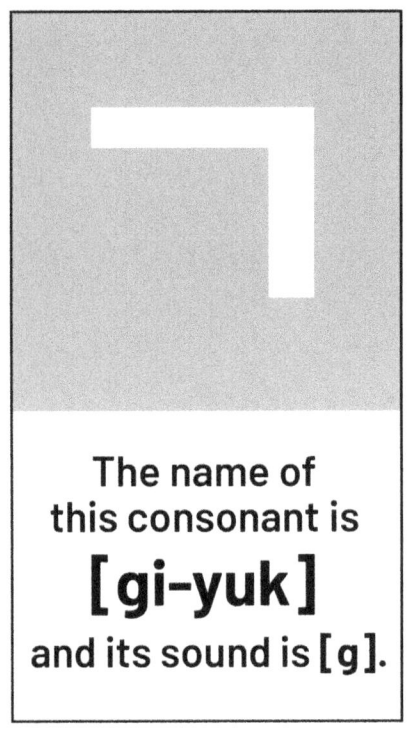

The name of this consonant is

[gi-yuk]

and its sound is [g].

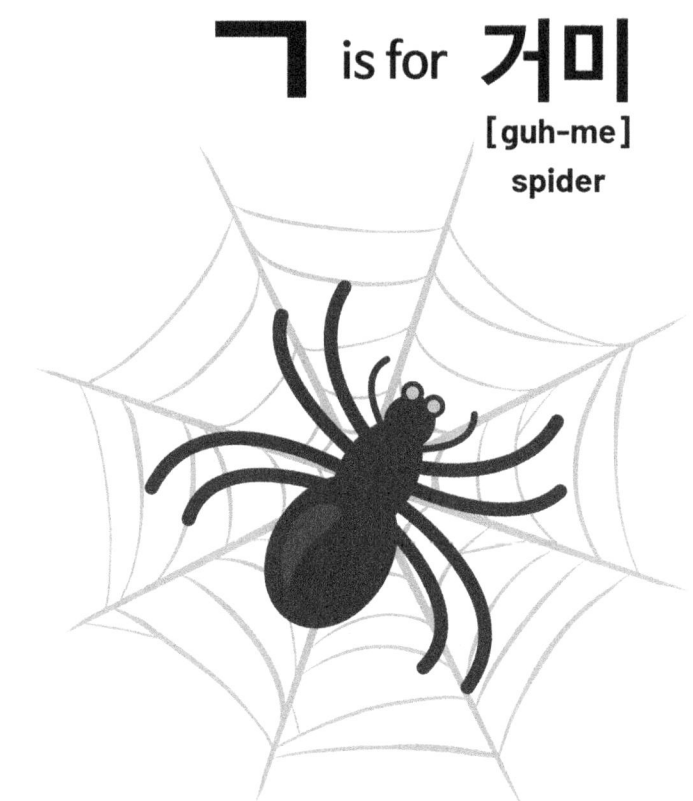

ㄱ is for 거미

[guh-me]

spider

Start on the dot. Trace the dotted line. Use the arrow as a guide.

①

①

①

Trace it! Start at the dot! Write it!

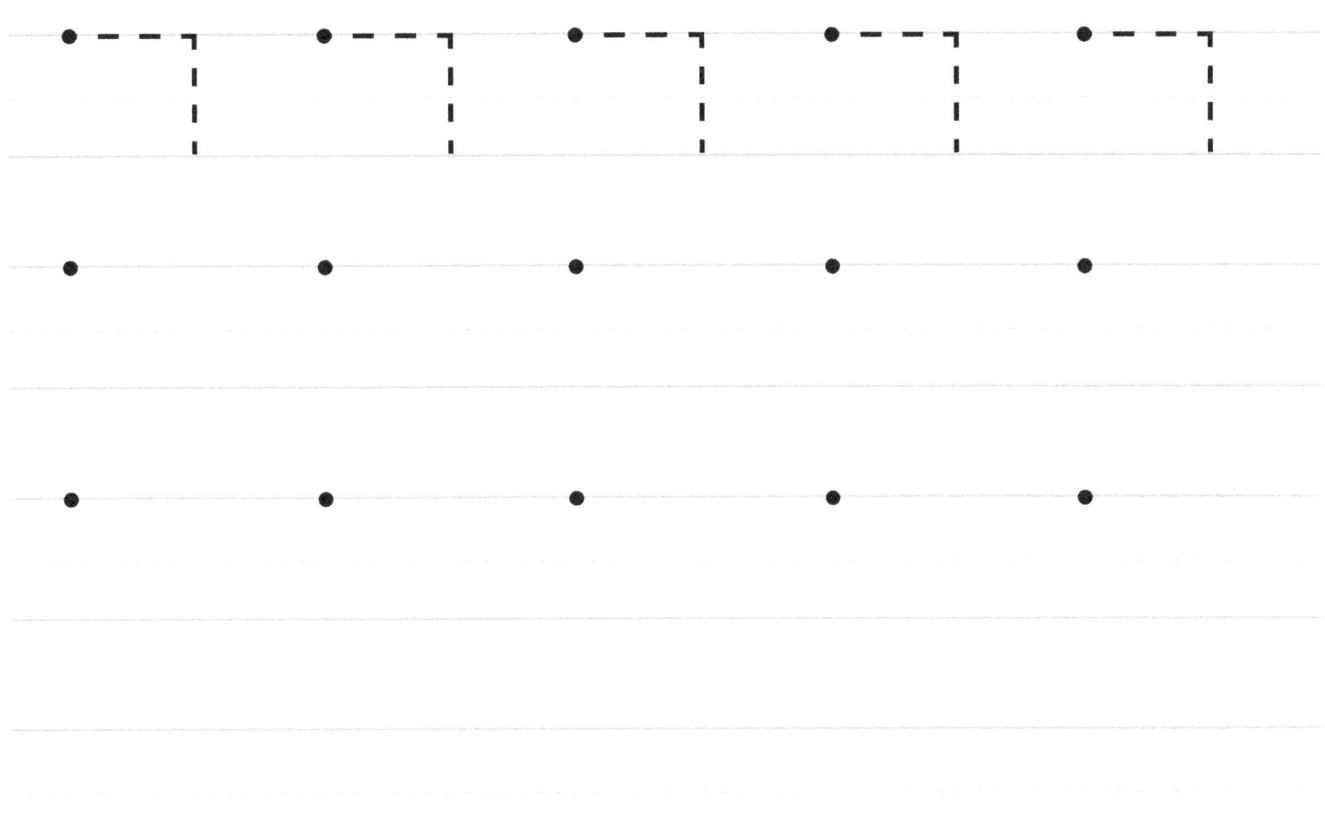

Trace the letter. Trace the word.

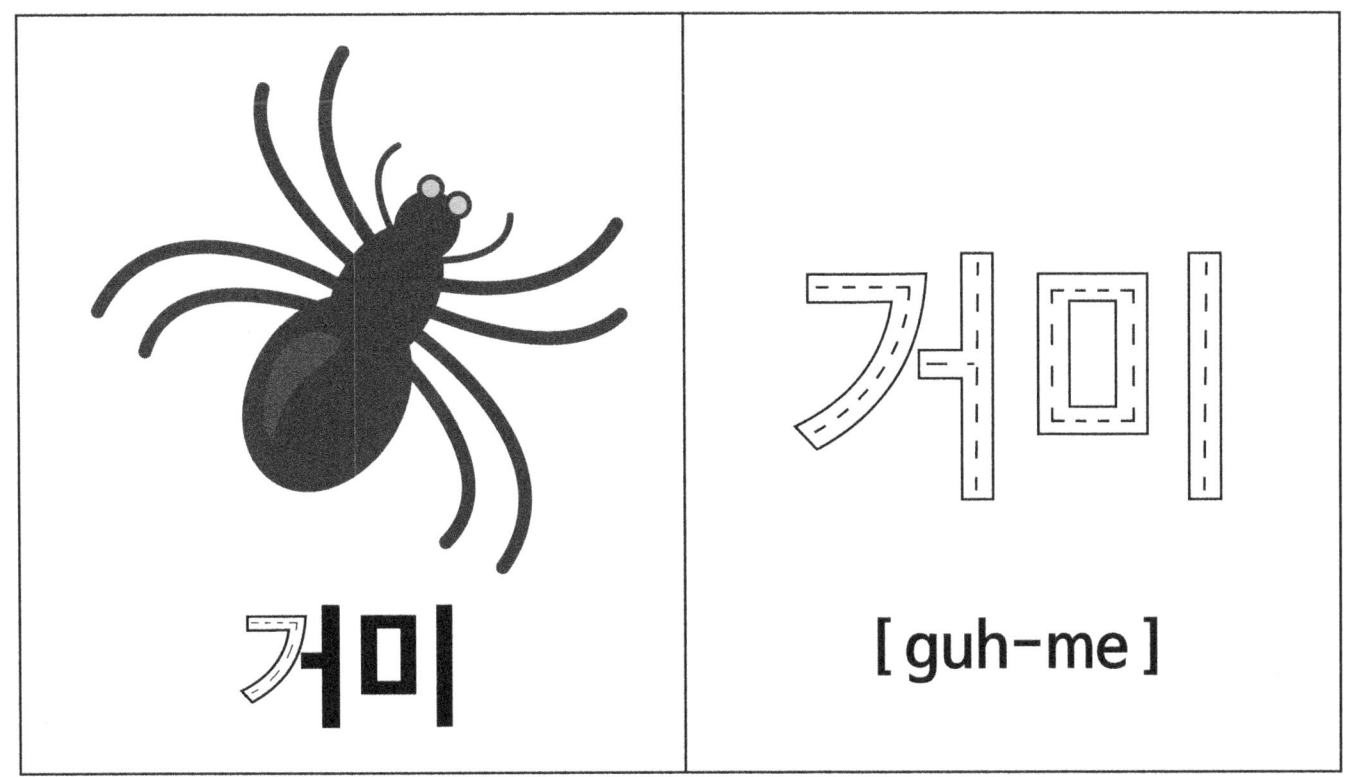

[guh-me]

ㄴ

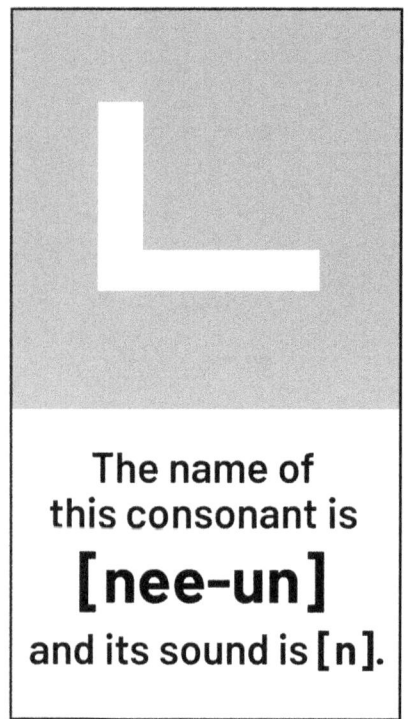

The name of this consonant is **[nee-un]** and its sound is **[n]**.

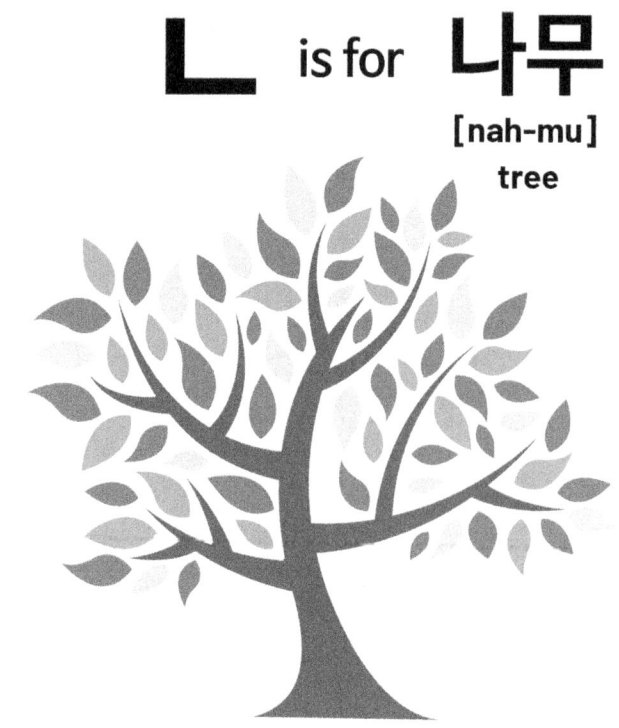

ㄴ is for 나무

[nah-mu]
tree

Start on the dot. Trace the dotted line. Use the arrow as a guide.

①

①

①

Trace it! Start at the dot! Write it!

Trace the letter. Trace the word.

[na-muh]

The name of this consonant is **[dee-gut]** and its sound is **[d]**.

ㄷ is for 다리미
[da-ree-me]
iron

Start on the dot. Trace the dotted line. Use the arrow as a guide.

Trace it! Start at the dot! Write it!

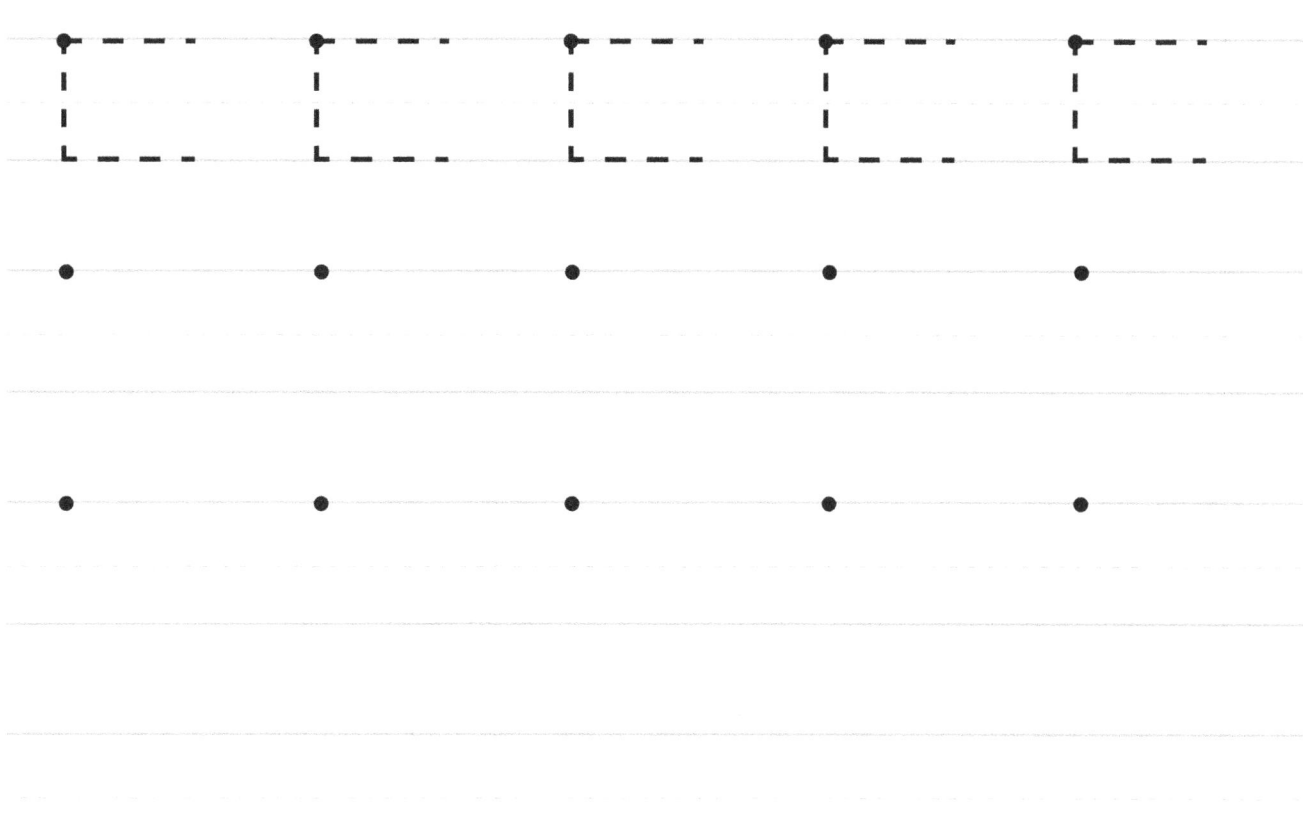

Trace the letter. Trace the word.

[da-ree-me]

The name of this consonant is **[ree-eul]** and its sound is [r].

ㄹ is for 로봇
[ro-bot]
robot

Start on the dot. Trace the dotted line. Use the arrow as a guide.

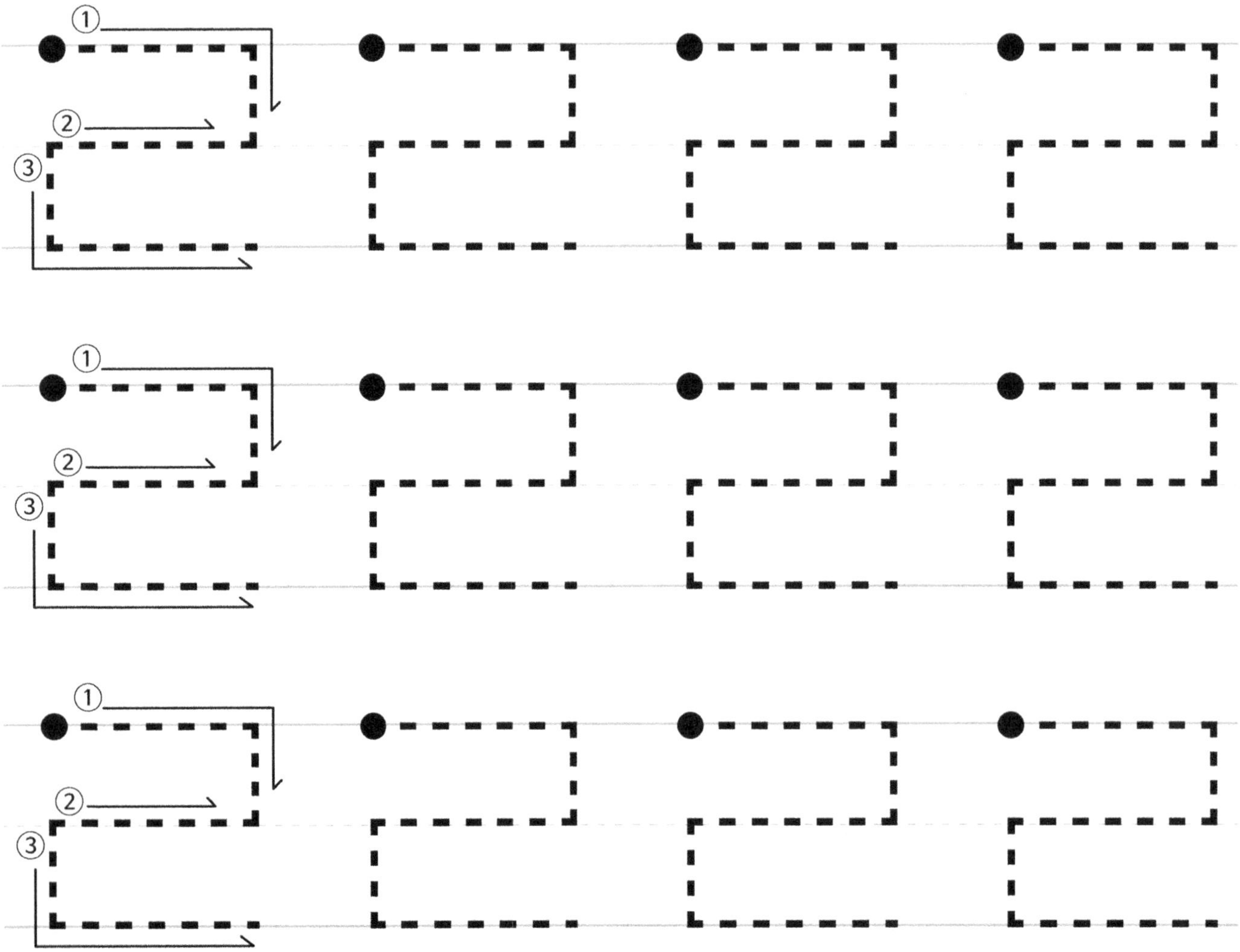

Trace it! Start at the dot! Write it!

Trace the letter. Trace the word.

[ro-bot]

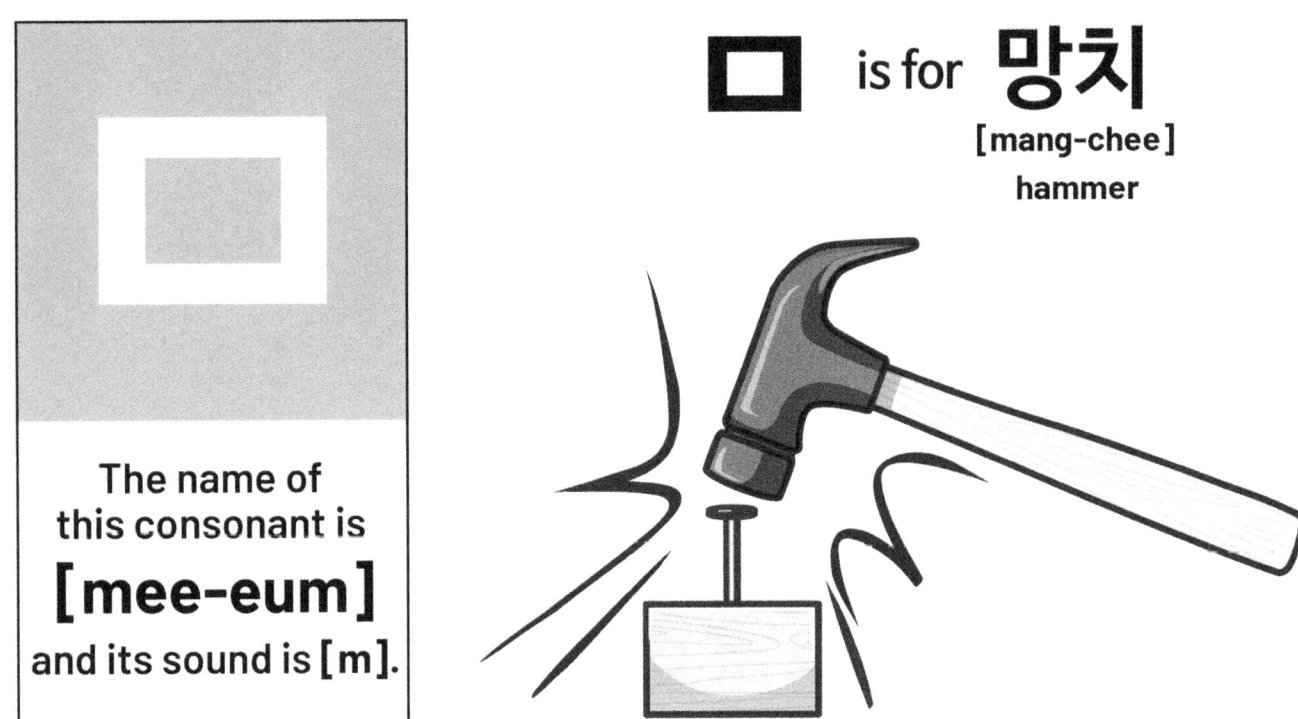

ㅁ is for 망치
[mang-chee]
hammer

The name of this consonant is **[mee-eum]** and its sound is **[m]**.

Start on the dot. Trace the dotted line. Use the arrow as a guide.

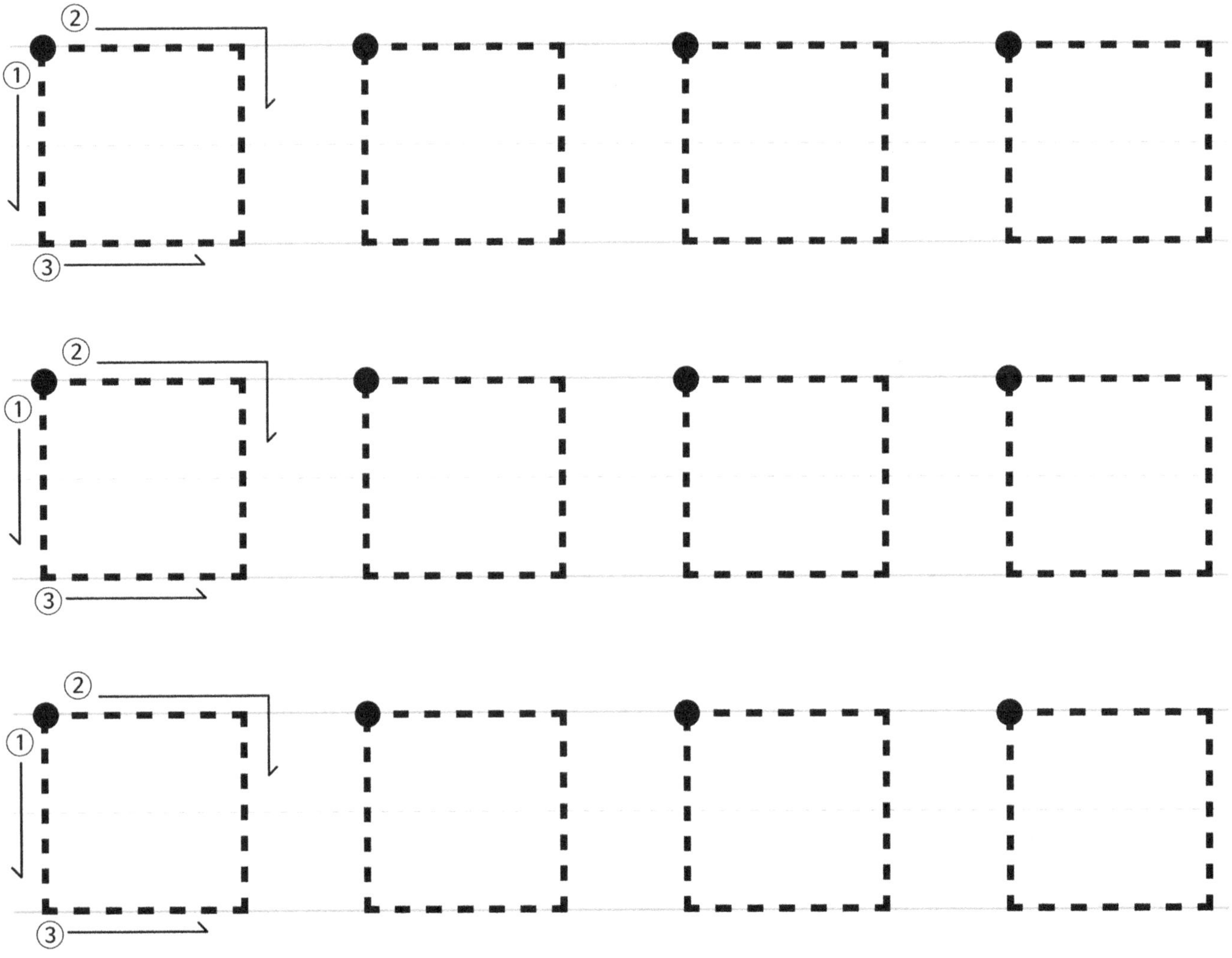

Trace it! Start at the dot! Write it!

Trace the letter. Trace the word.

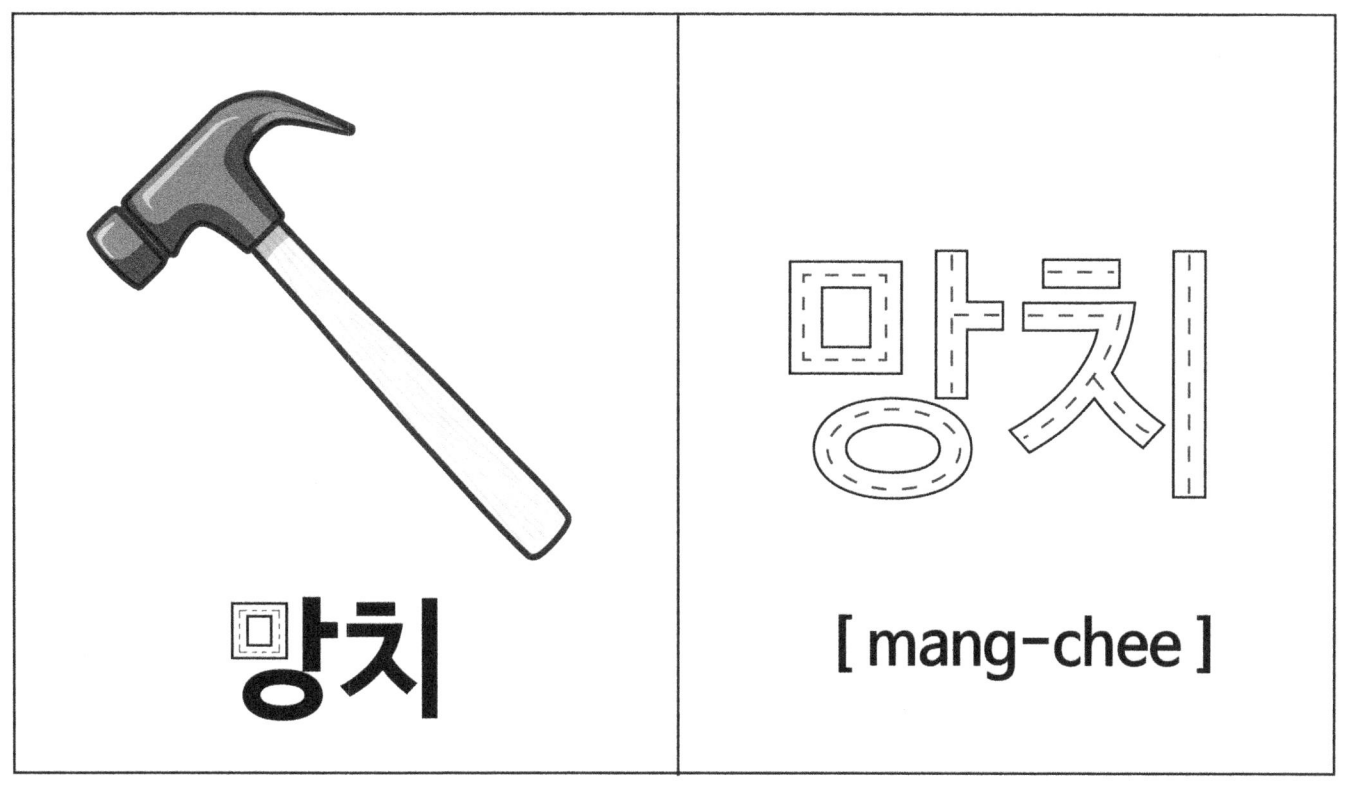

망치

[mang-chee]

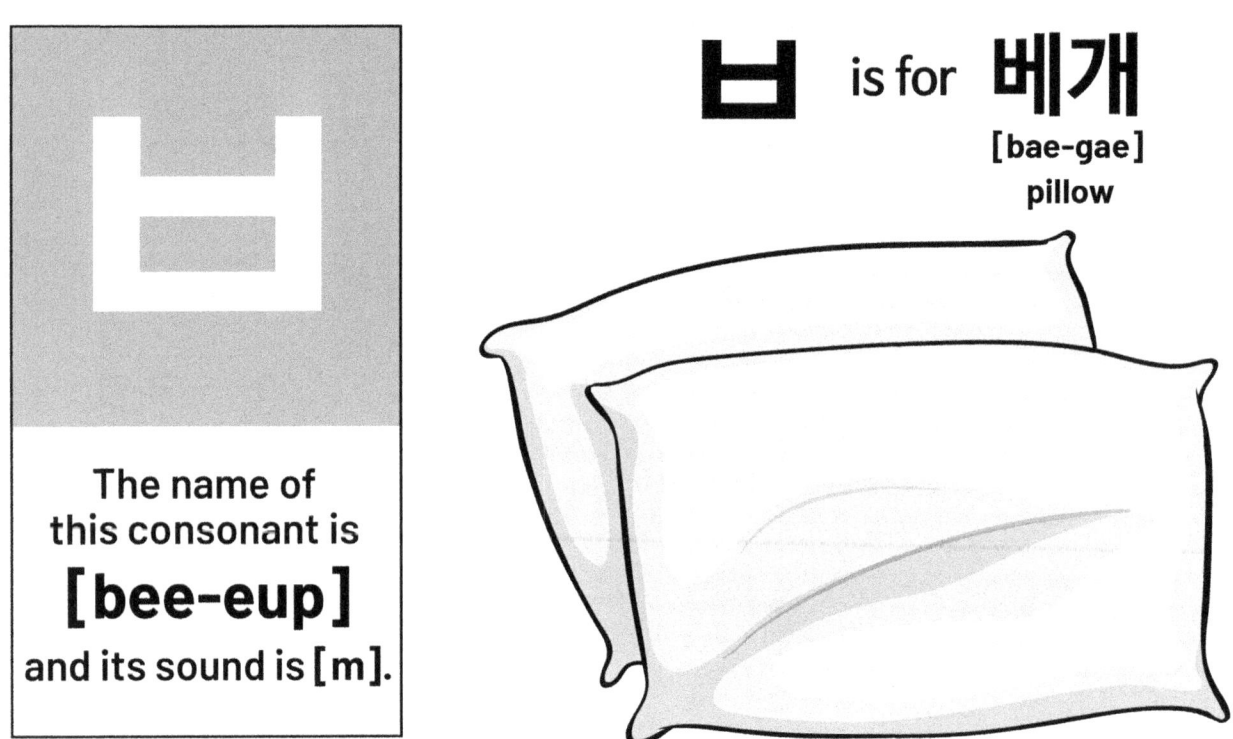

ㅂ is for 베개
[bae-gae]
pillow

The name of this consonant is **[bee-eup]** and its sound is **[m]**.

Start on the dot. Trace the dotted line. Use the arrow as a guide.

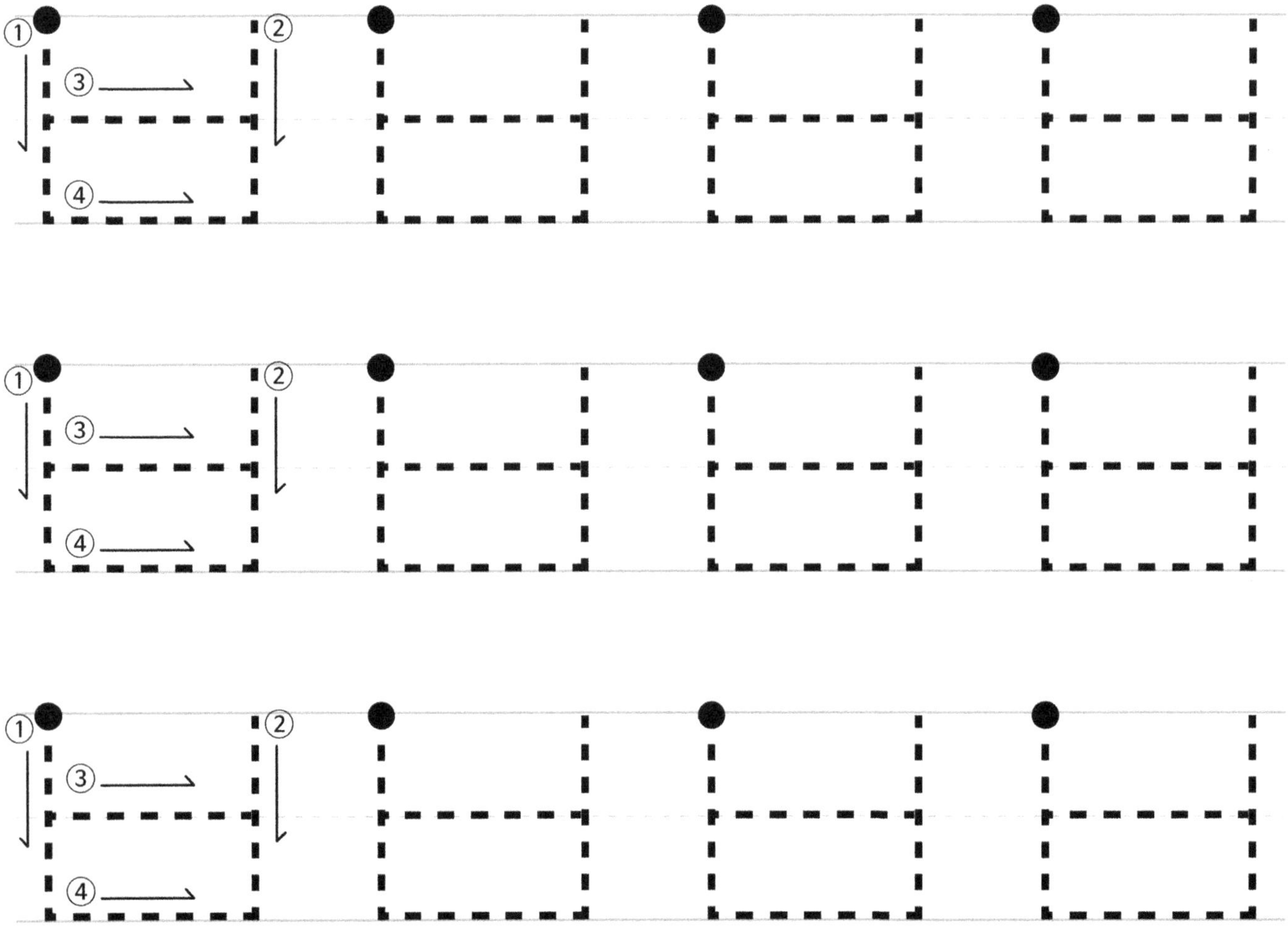

Trace it! Start at the dot! Write it!

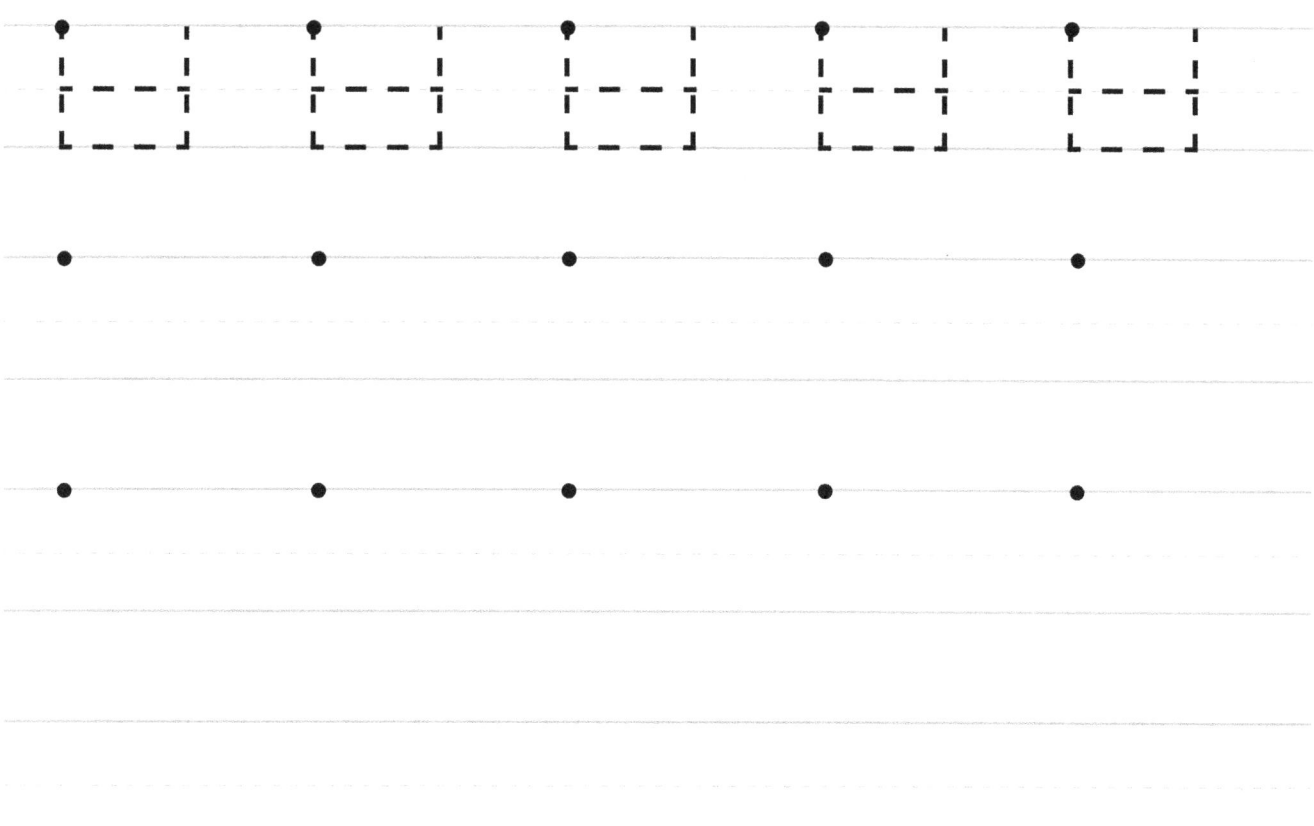

Trace the letter. Trace the word.

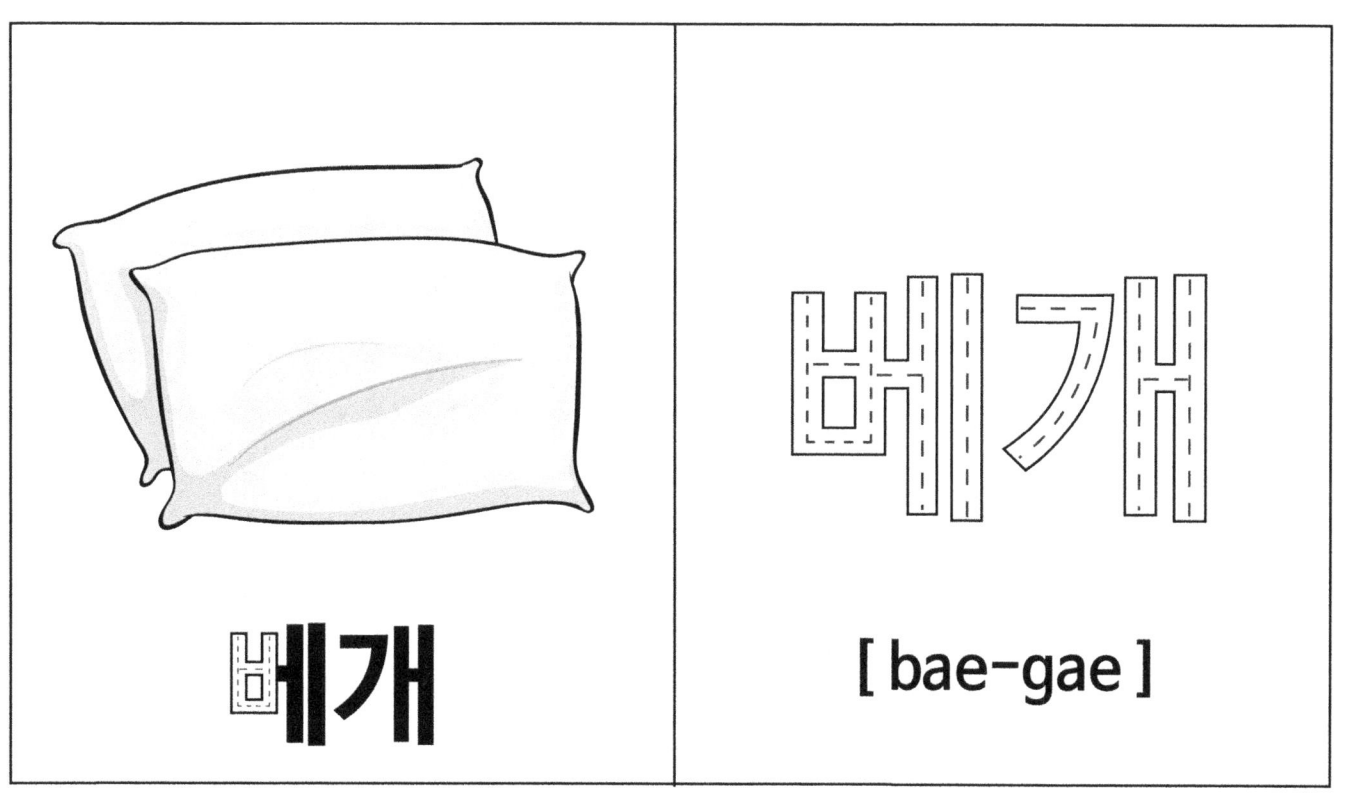

베개

[bae-gae]

The name of this consonant is **[shee-ot]** and its sound is [s].

ㅅ is for 수박
[su-bak]
watermelon

Start on the dot. Trace the dotted line. Use the arrow as a guide.

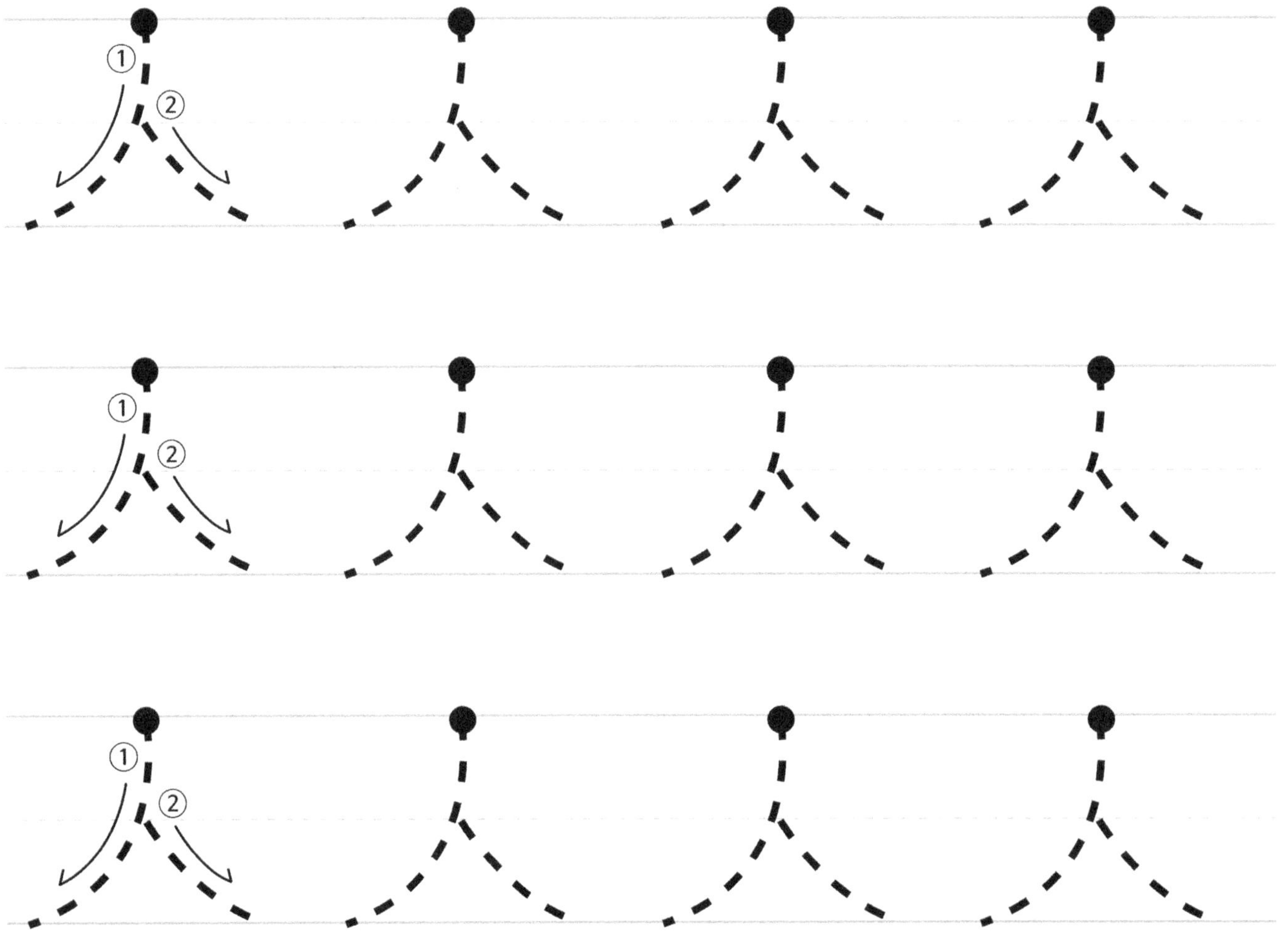

Trace it! Start at the dot! Write it!

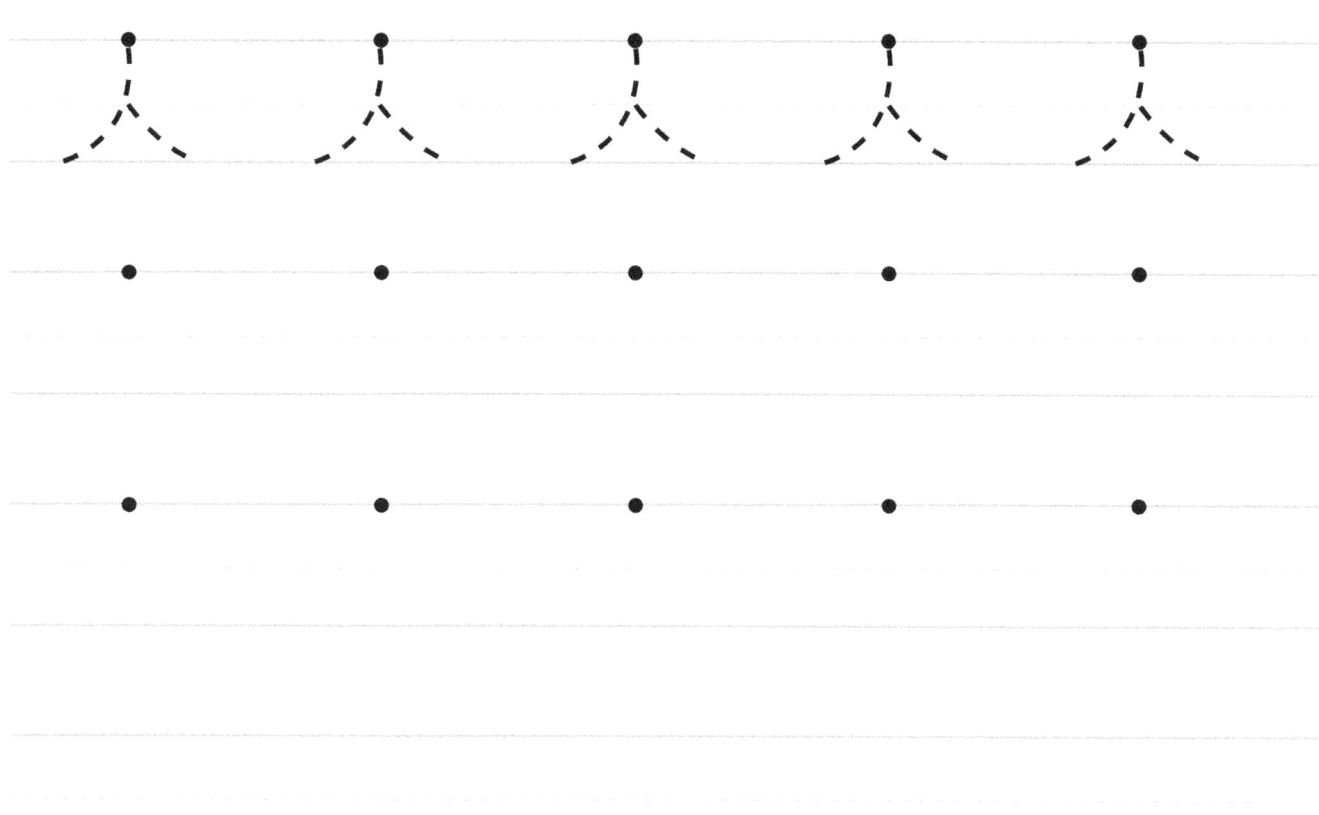

Trace the letter. Trace the word.

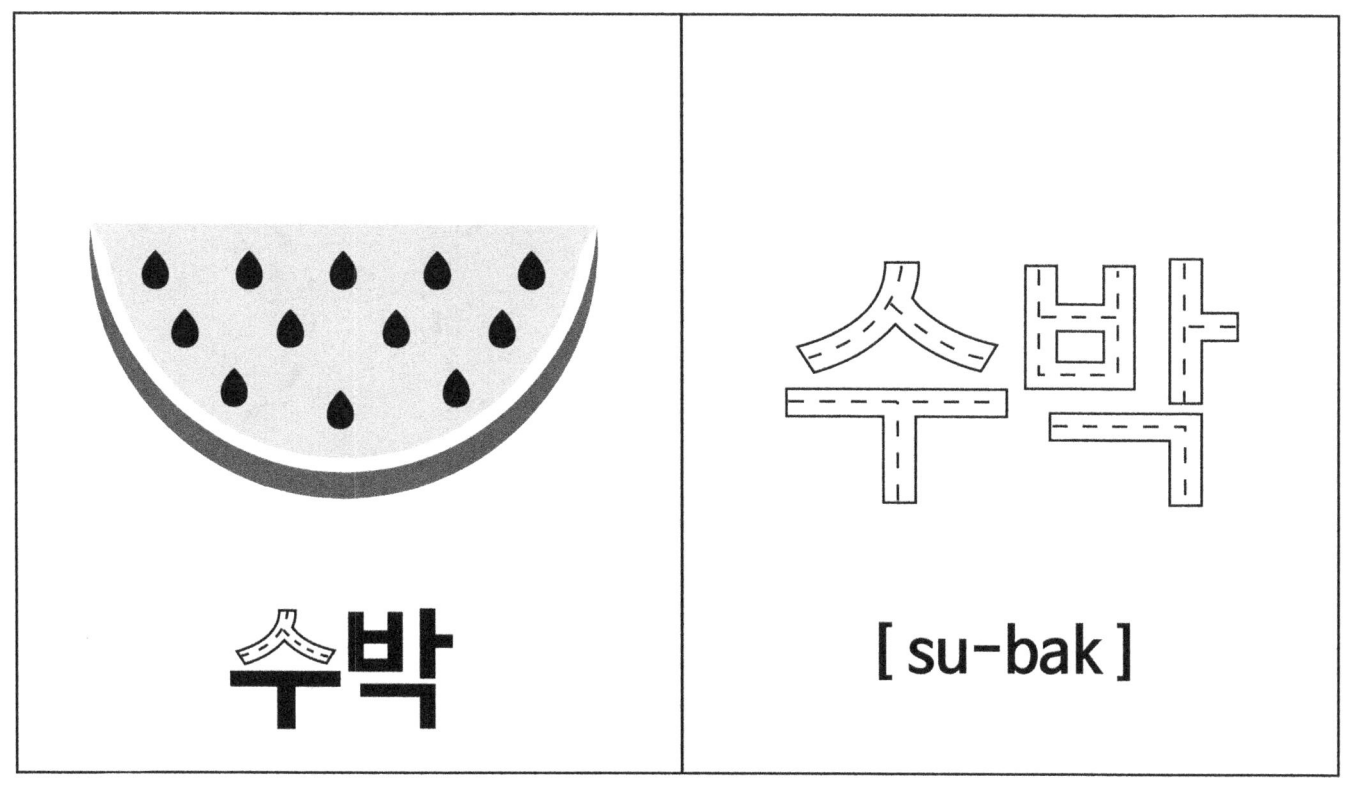

수박

[su-bak]

The name of this consonant is **[ee-eung]** and its has no sound.

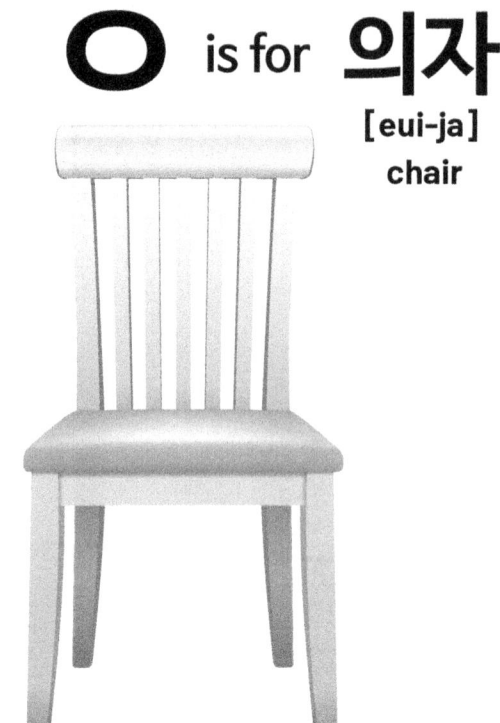

ㅇ is for 의자
[eui-ja]
chair

Start on the dot. Trace the dotted line. Use the arrow as a guide.

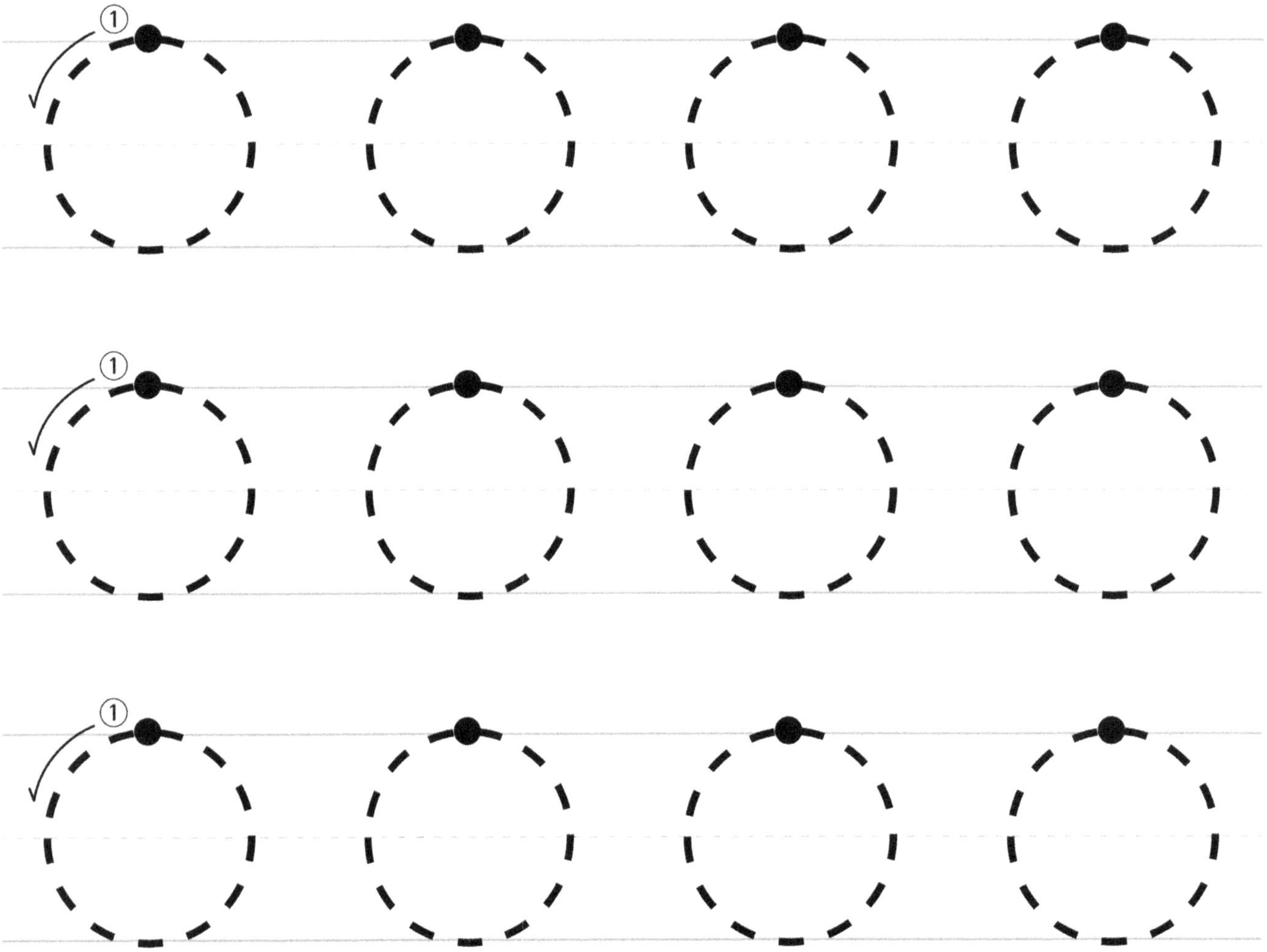

Trace it! Start at the dot! Write it!

Trace the letter. Trace the word.

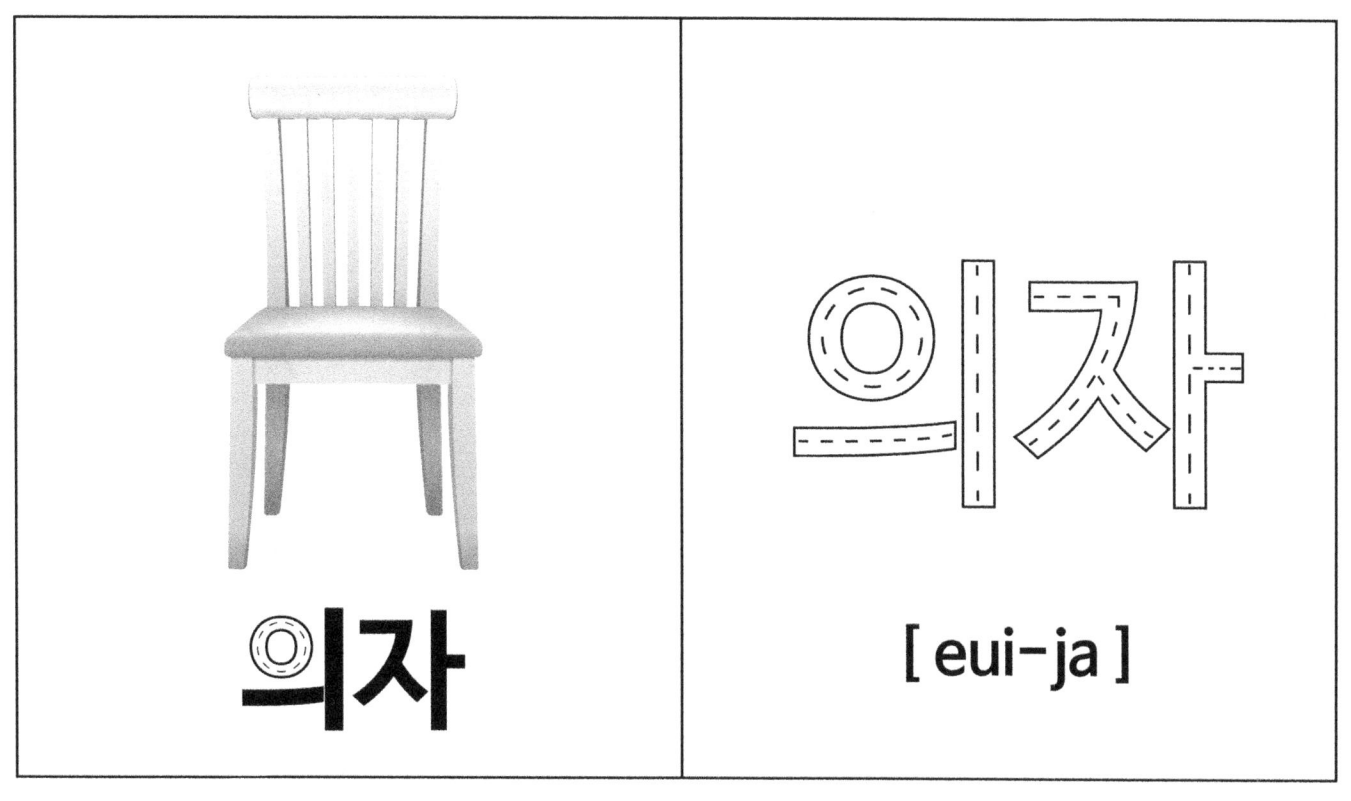

의자

[eui-ja]

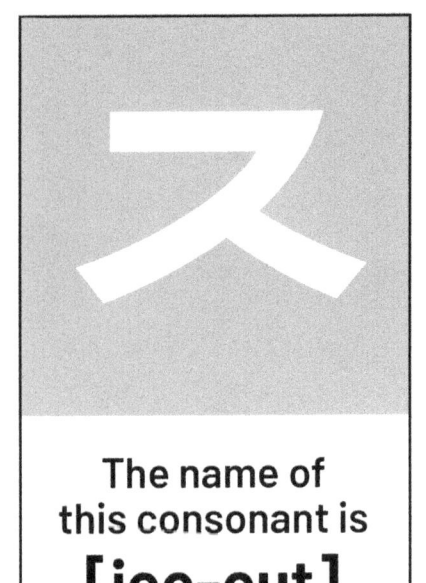

ㅈ is for 자전거
[ja-jun-guh]
bicycle

The name of this consonant is **[jee-eut]** and its sound is [j].

Start on the dot. Trace the dotted line. Use the arrow as a guide.

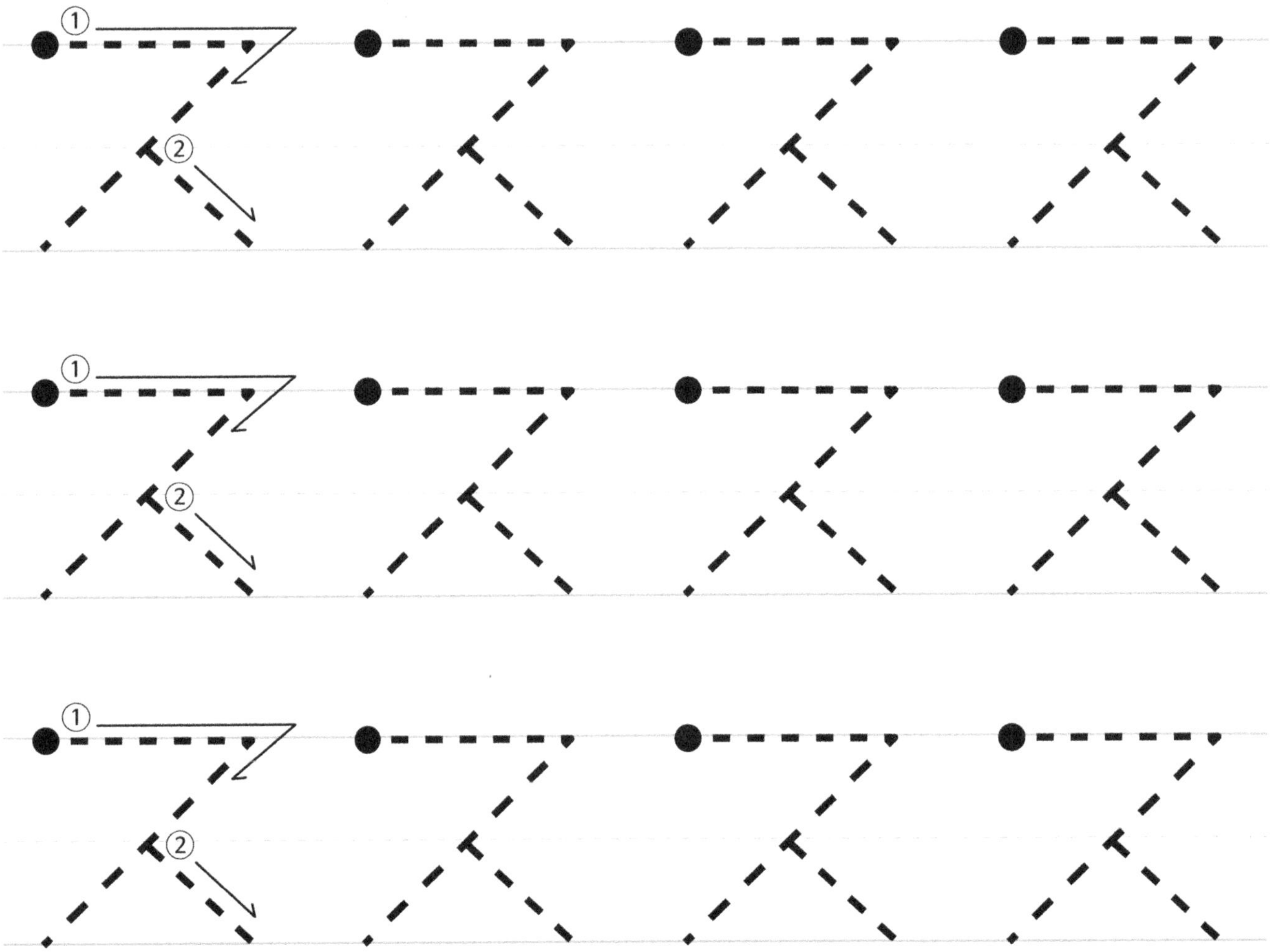

Trace it! Start at the dot! Write it!

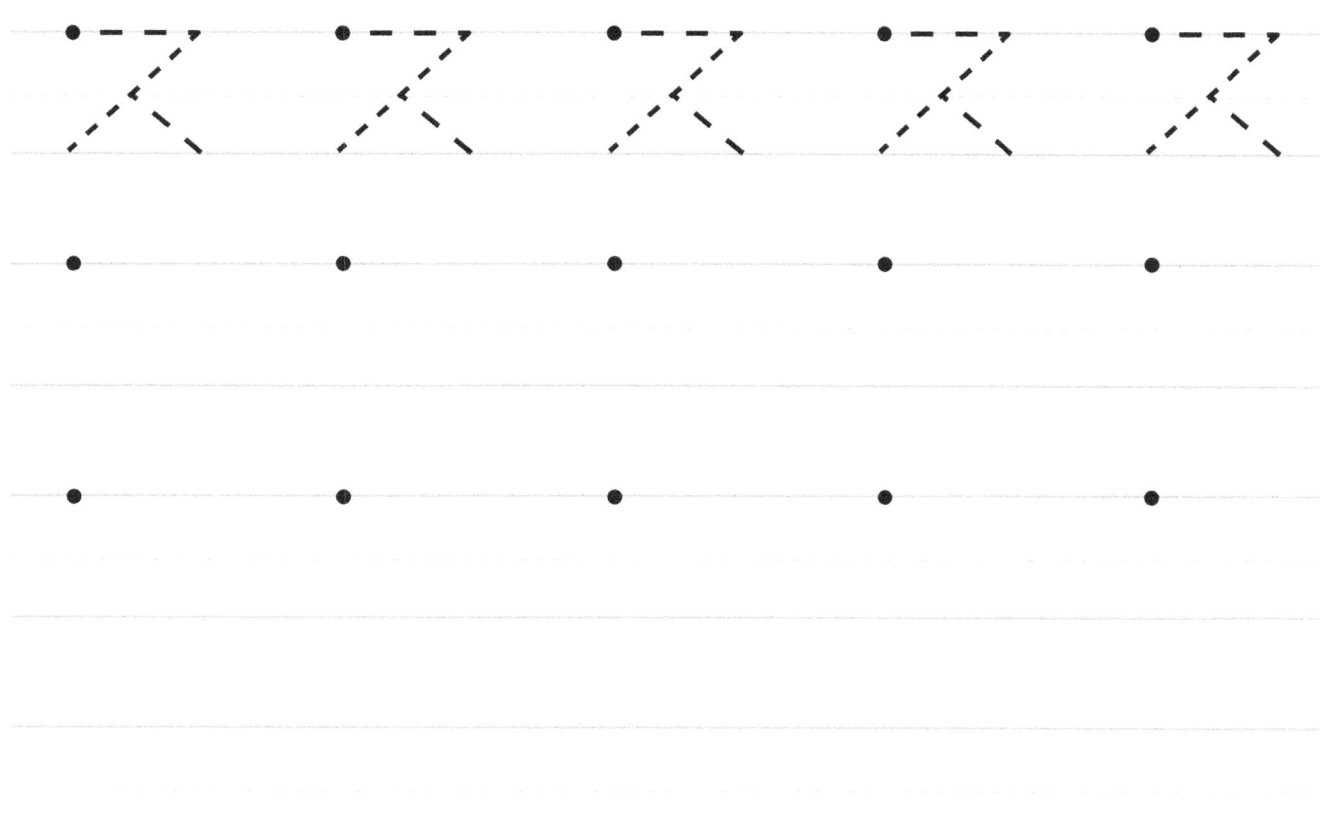

Trace the letter. Trace the word.

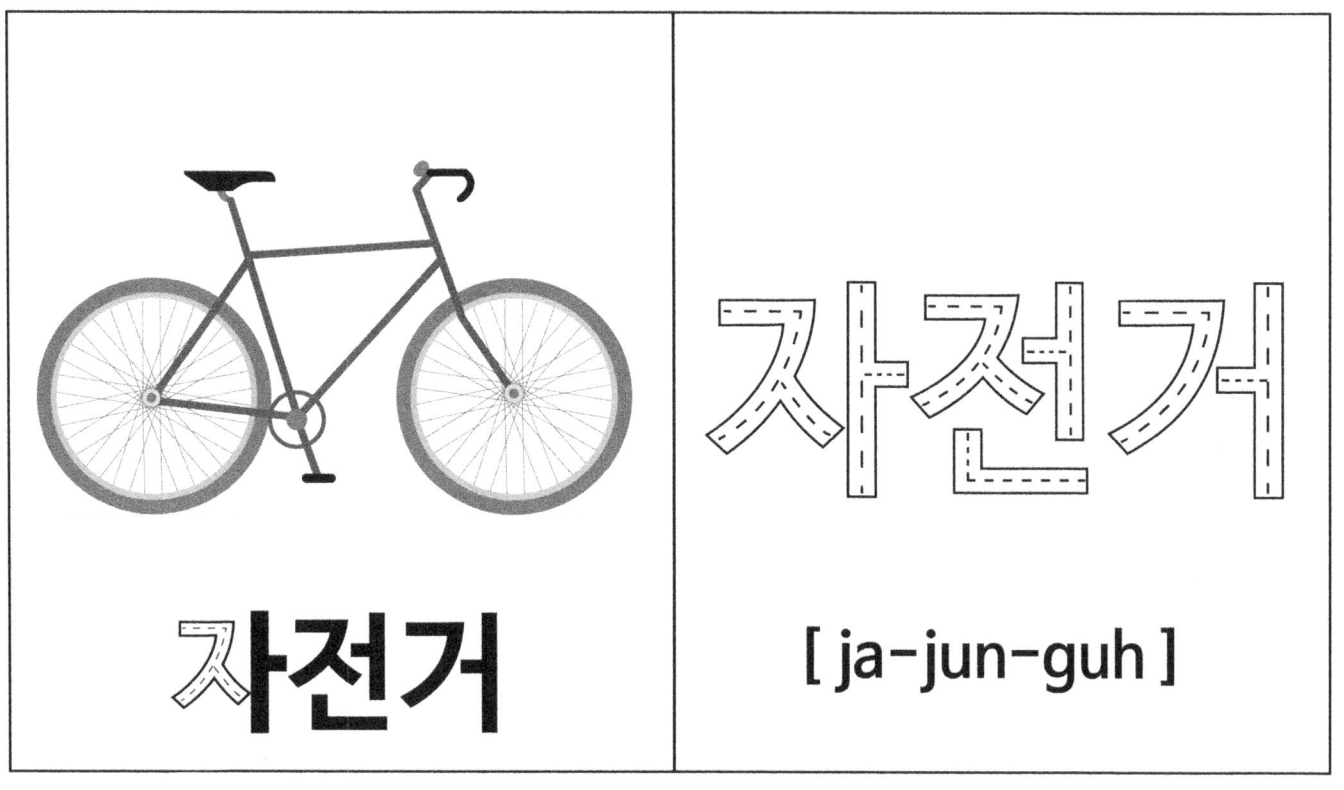

자전거

[ja-jun-guh]

ㅊ is for 침대
[chim-dae]
bed

The name of this consonant is **[chee-eut]** and its sound is **[ch]**.

Start on the dot. Trace the dotted line. Use the arrow as a guide.

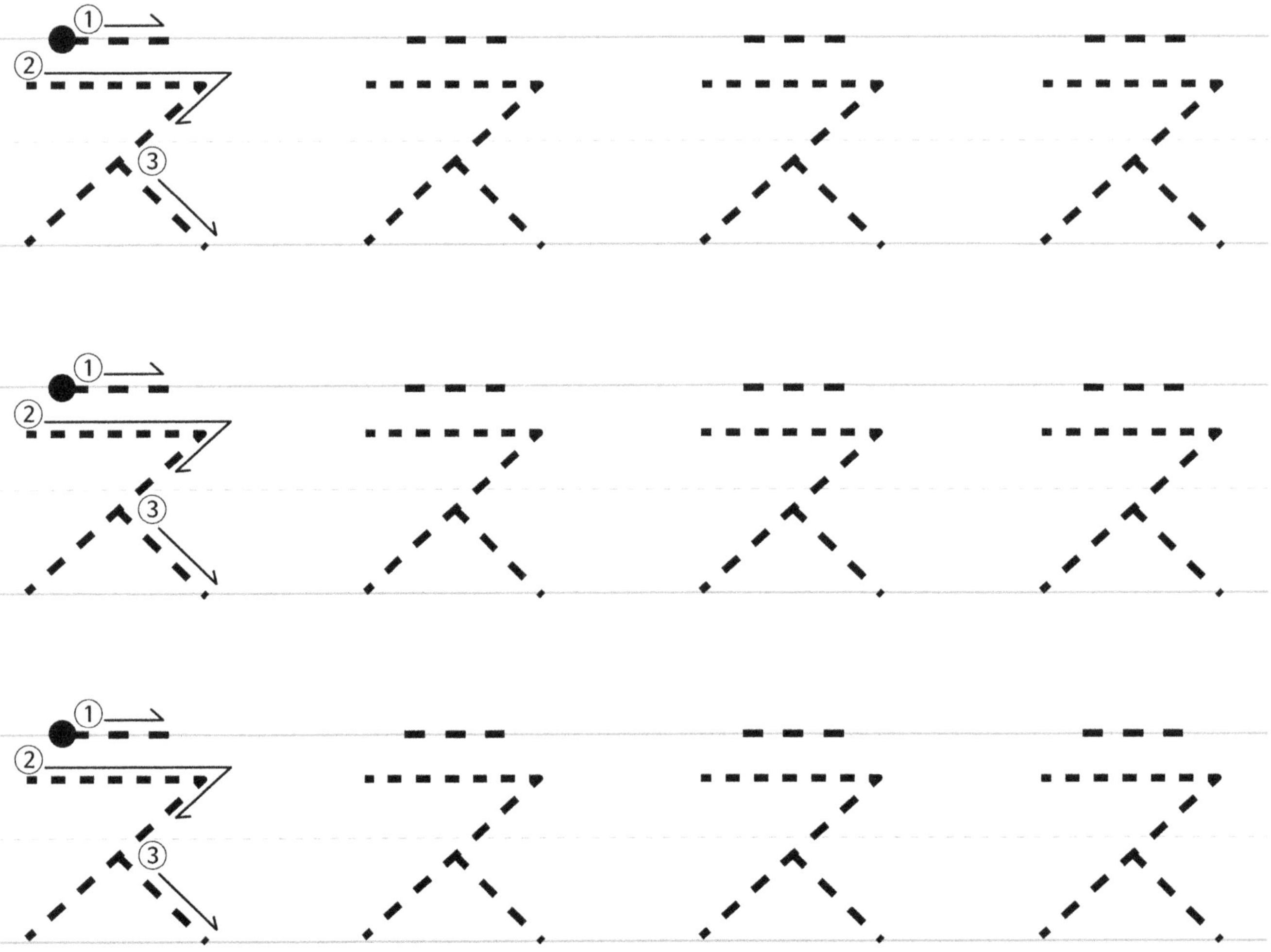

Trace it! Start at the dot! Write it!

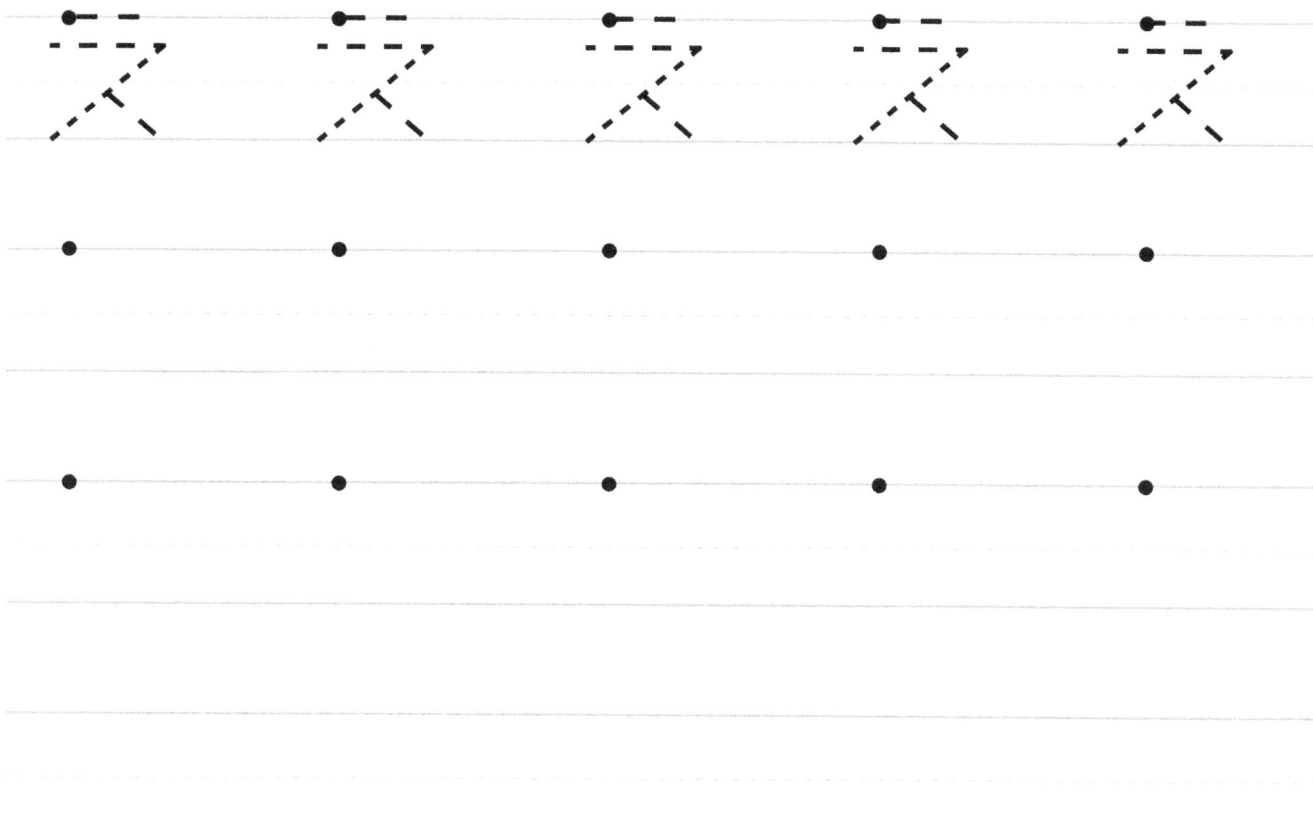

Trace the letter. Trace the word.

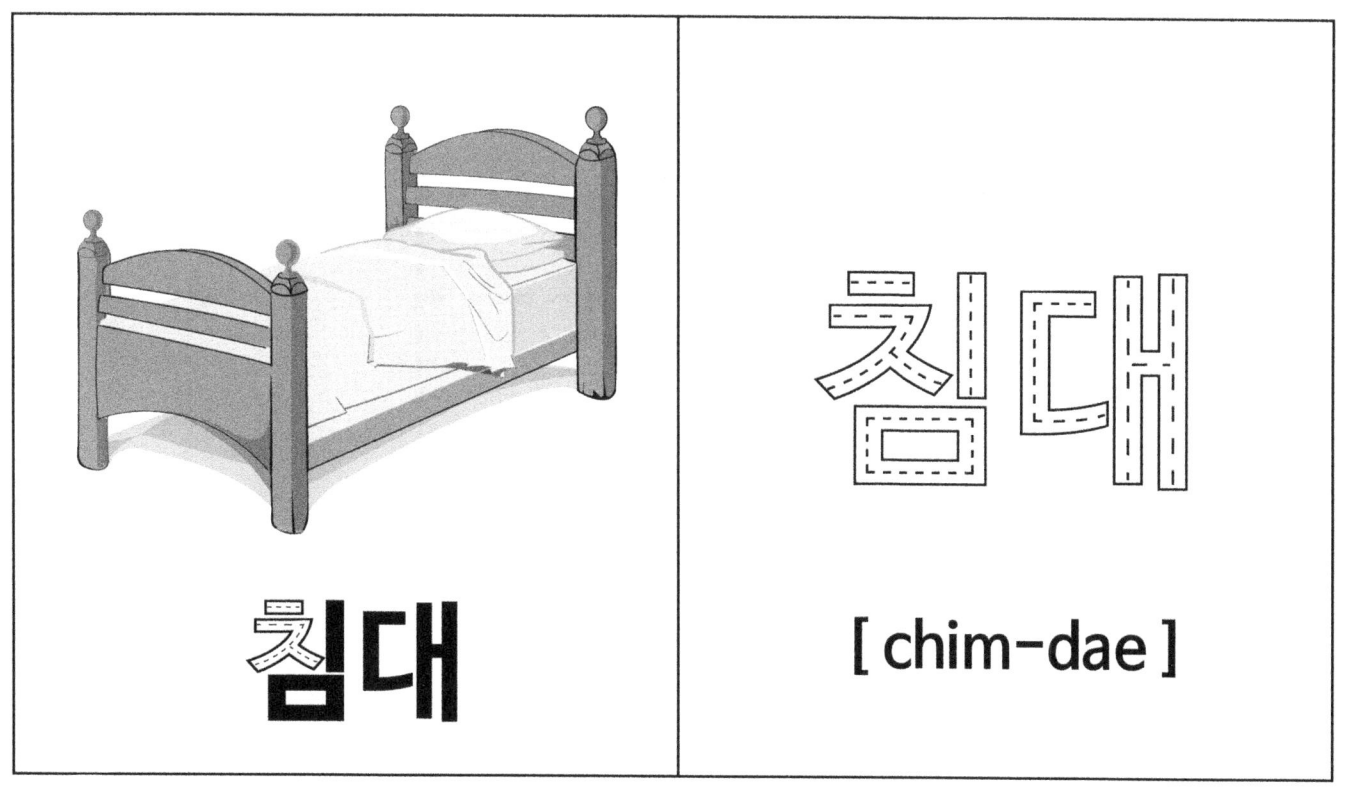

침대

[chim-dae]

ㅋ

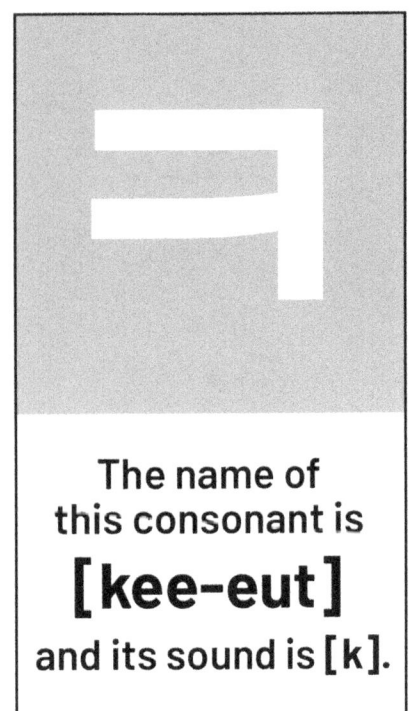

The name of
this consonant is
[kee-eut]
and its sound is [k].

ㅋ is for 카메라

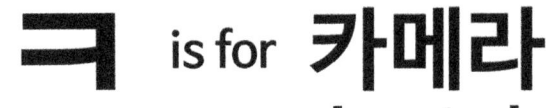

[ca-meh-ra]
camera

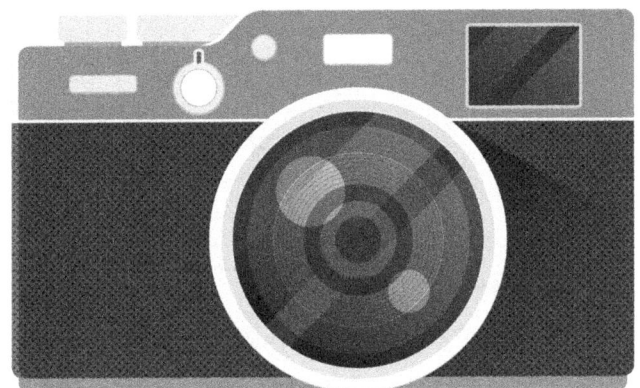

Start on the dot. Trace the dotted line. Use the arrow as a guide.

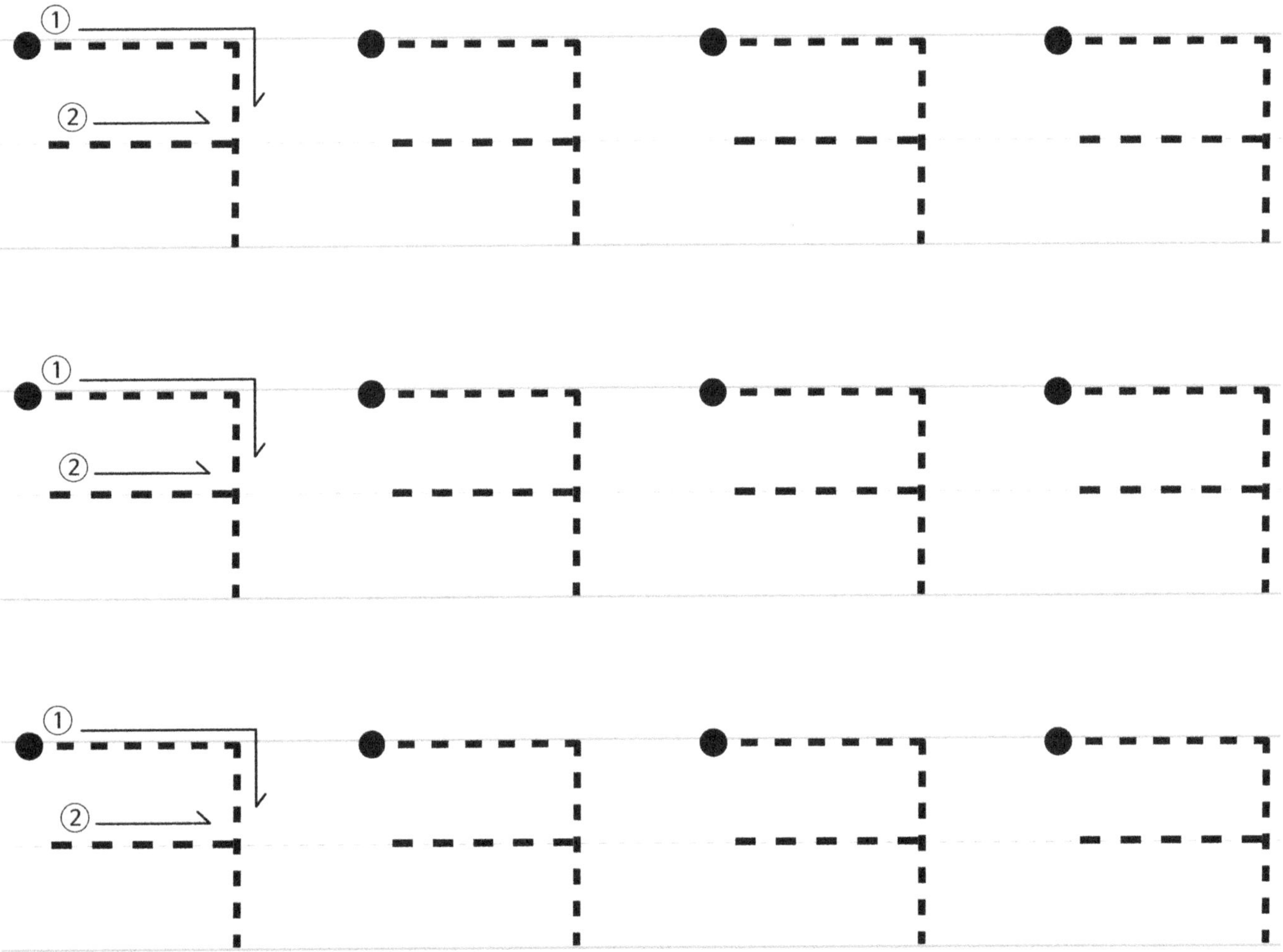

Trace it! Start at the dot! Write it!

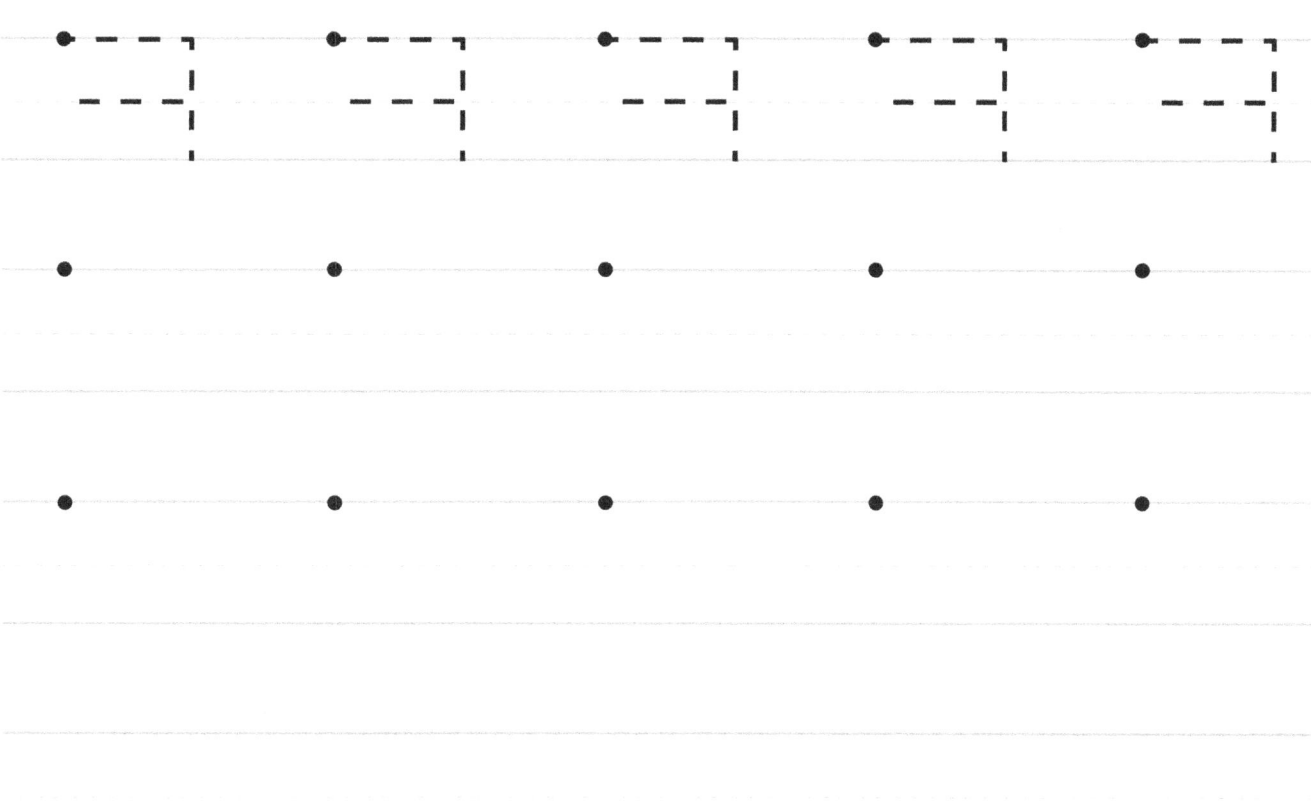

Trace the letter. Trace the word.

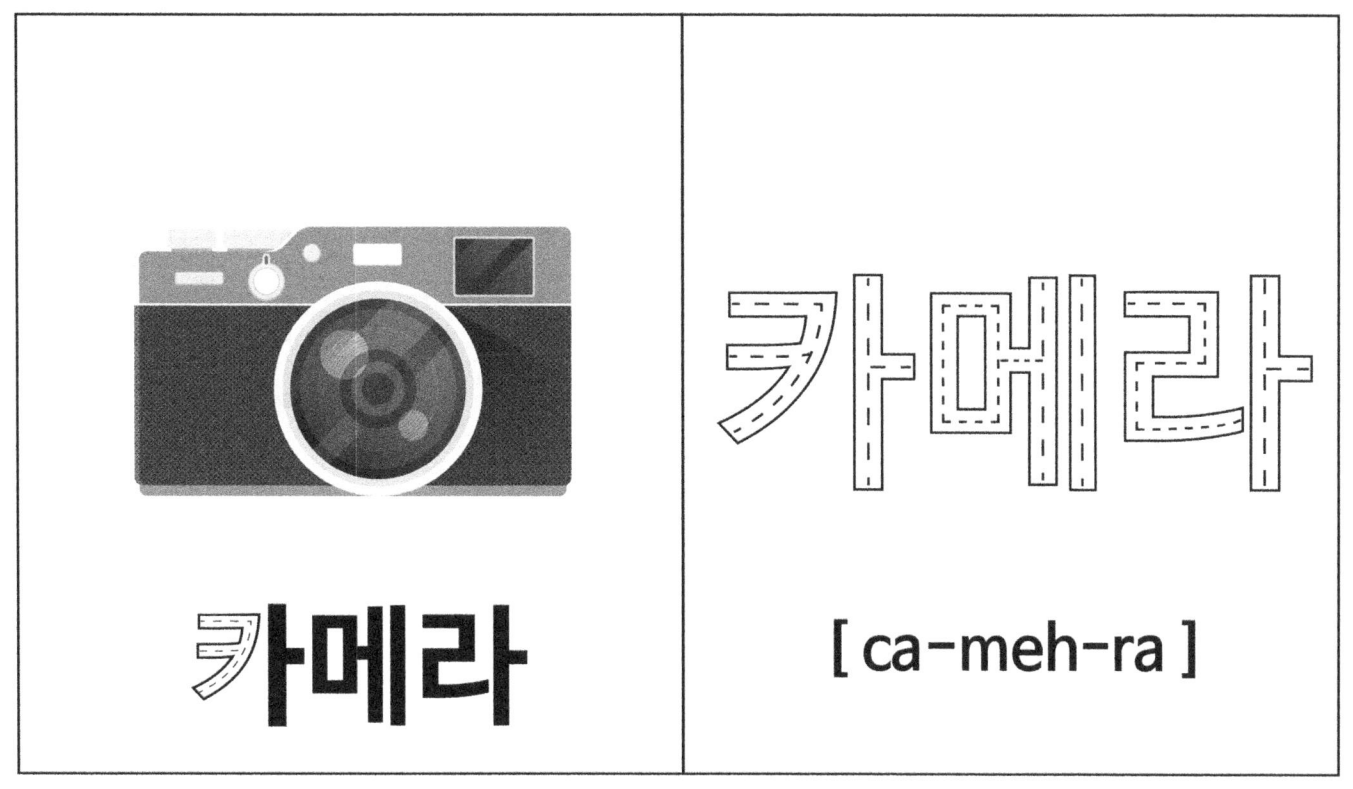

[ca-meh-ra]

ㅌ is for 토끼
[to-kki]
rabbit

The name of this consonant is

[tee-eut]

and its sound is [t].

Start on the dot. Trace the dotted line. Use the arrow as a guide.

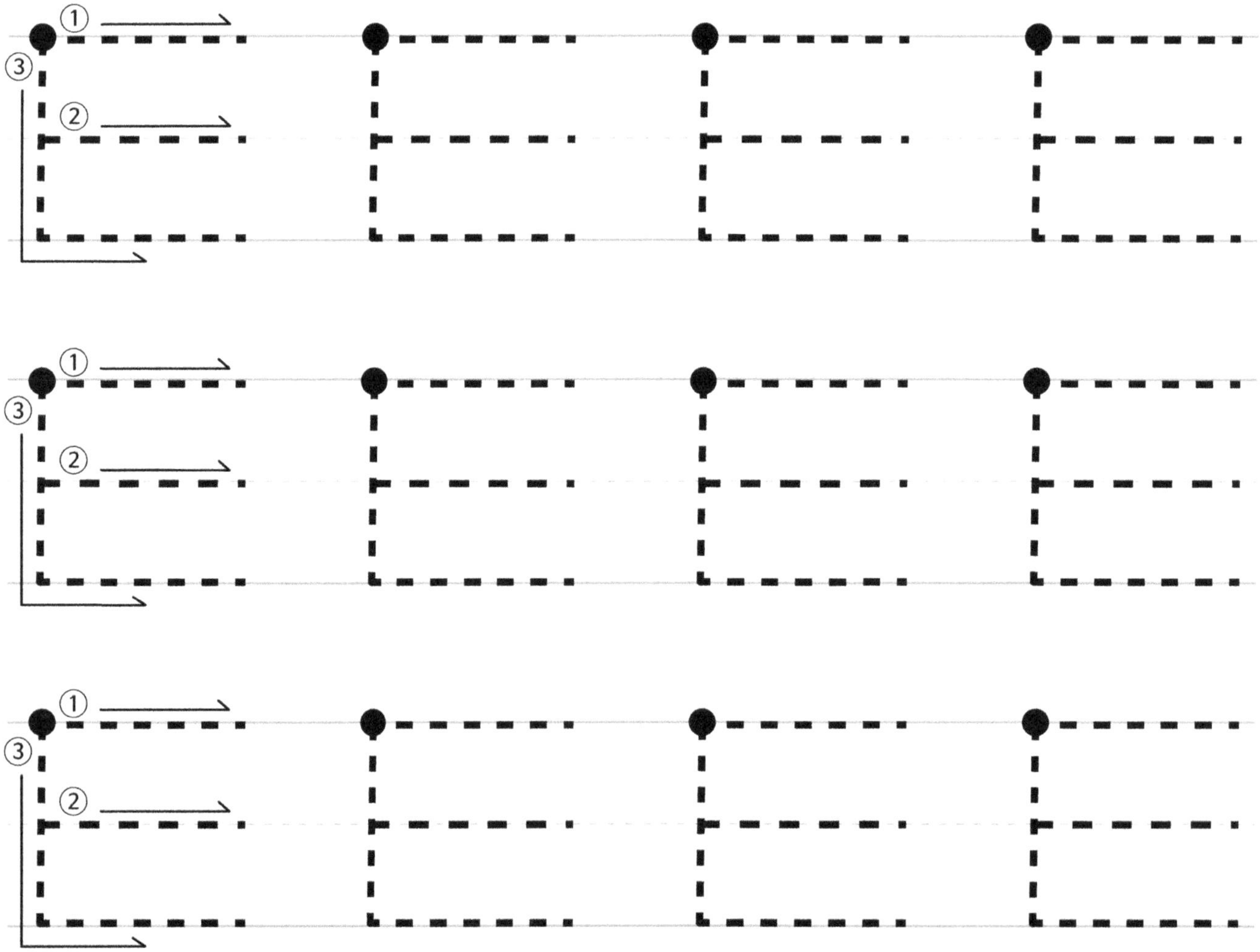

Trace it! Start at the dot! Write it!

Trace the letter. Trace the word.

토끼

[to-kki]

ㅍ is for 펭귄
[pang-gwin]
penguin

The name of this consonant is **[pee-eup]** and its sound is [p].

Start on the dot. Trace the dotted line. Use the arrow as a guide.

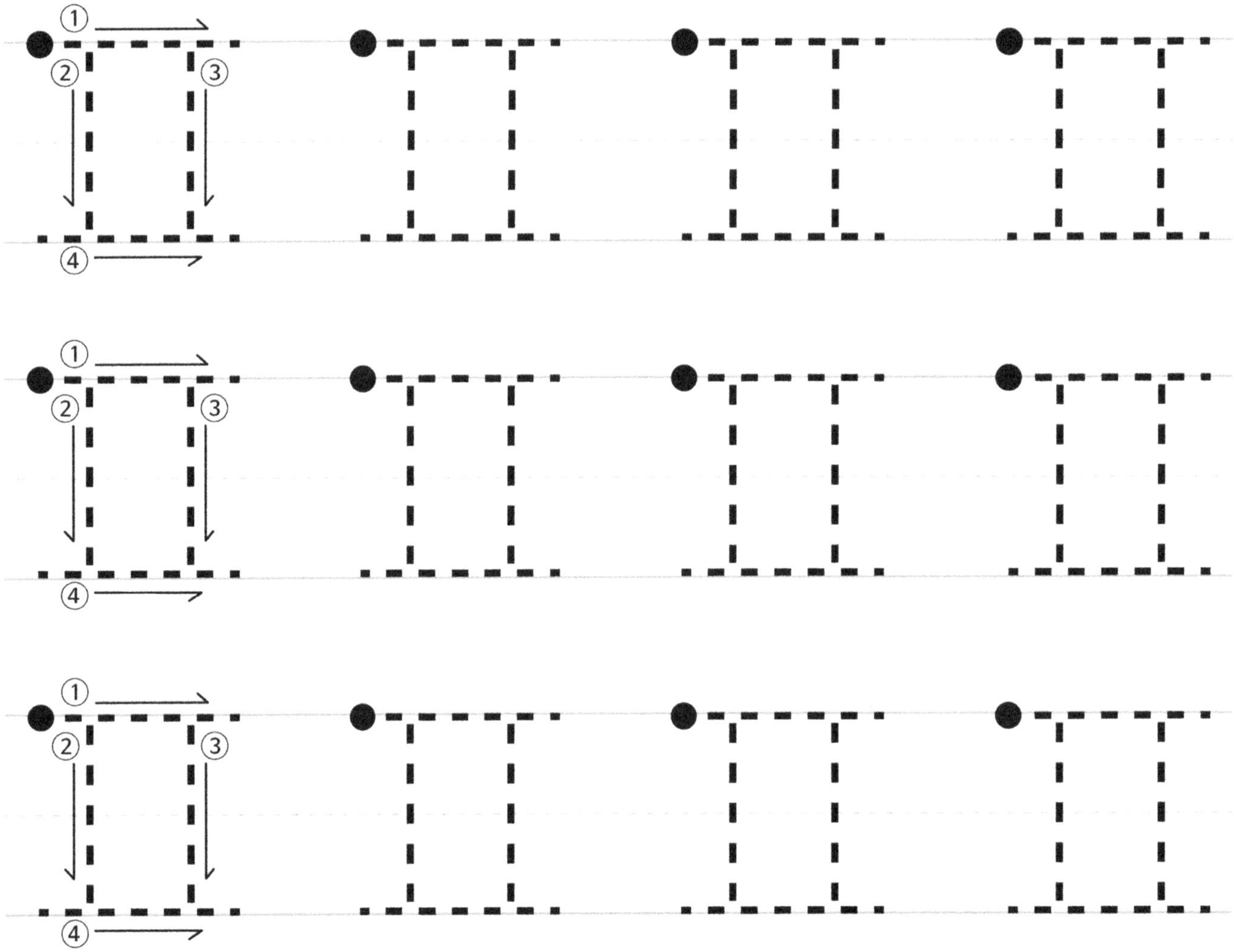

Trace it! Start at the dot! Write it!

ㅠ　ㅠ　ㅠ　ㅠ　ㅠ

Trace the letter. Trace the word.

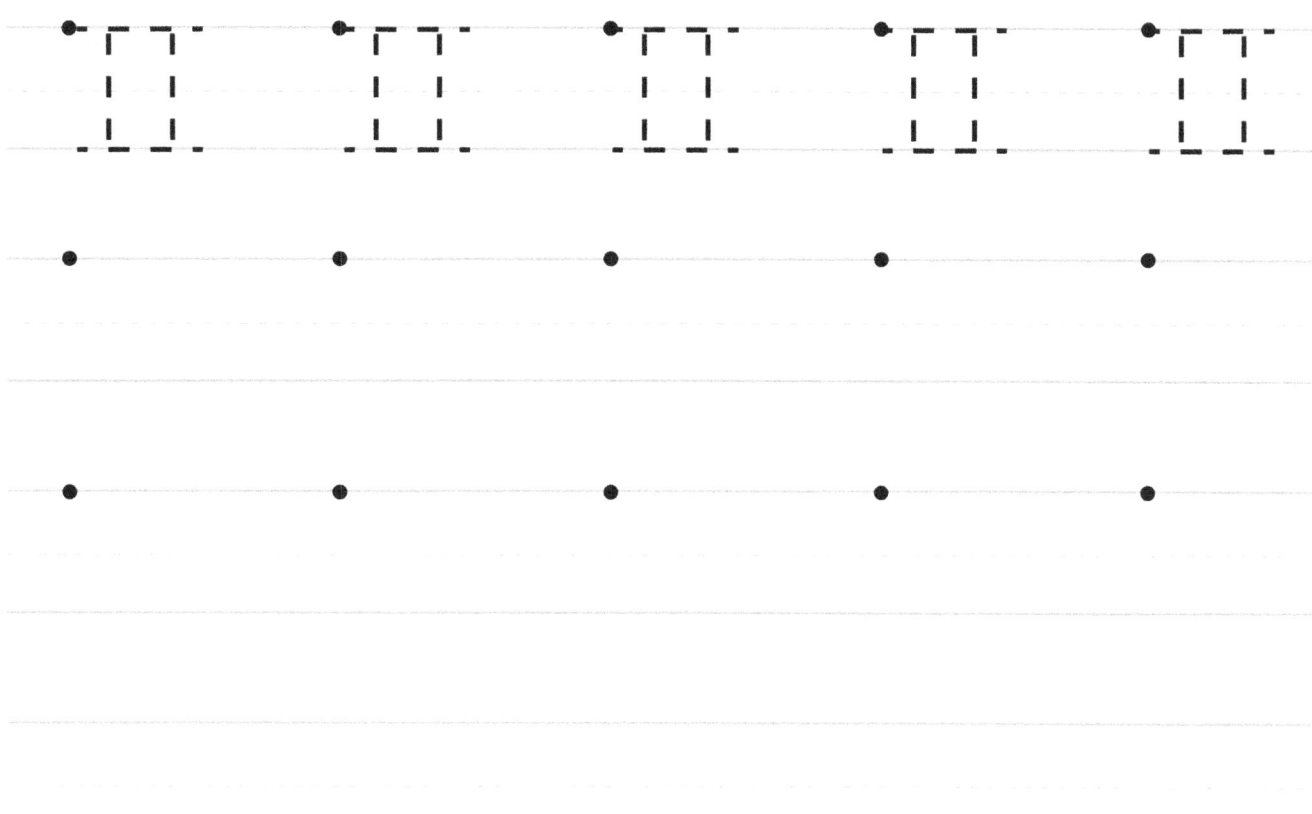

펭귄

[pang-gwin]

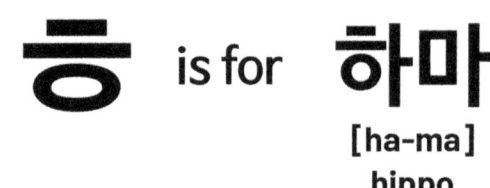 is for 하마
[ha-ma]
hippo

The name of this consonant is

[hee-eut]

and its sound is **[h]**.

Start on the dot. Trace the dotted line. Use the arrow as a guide.

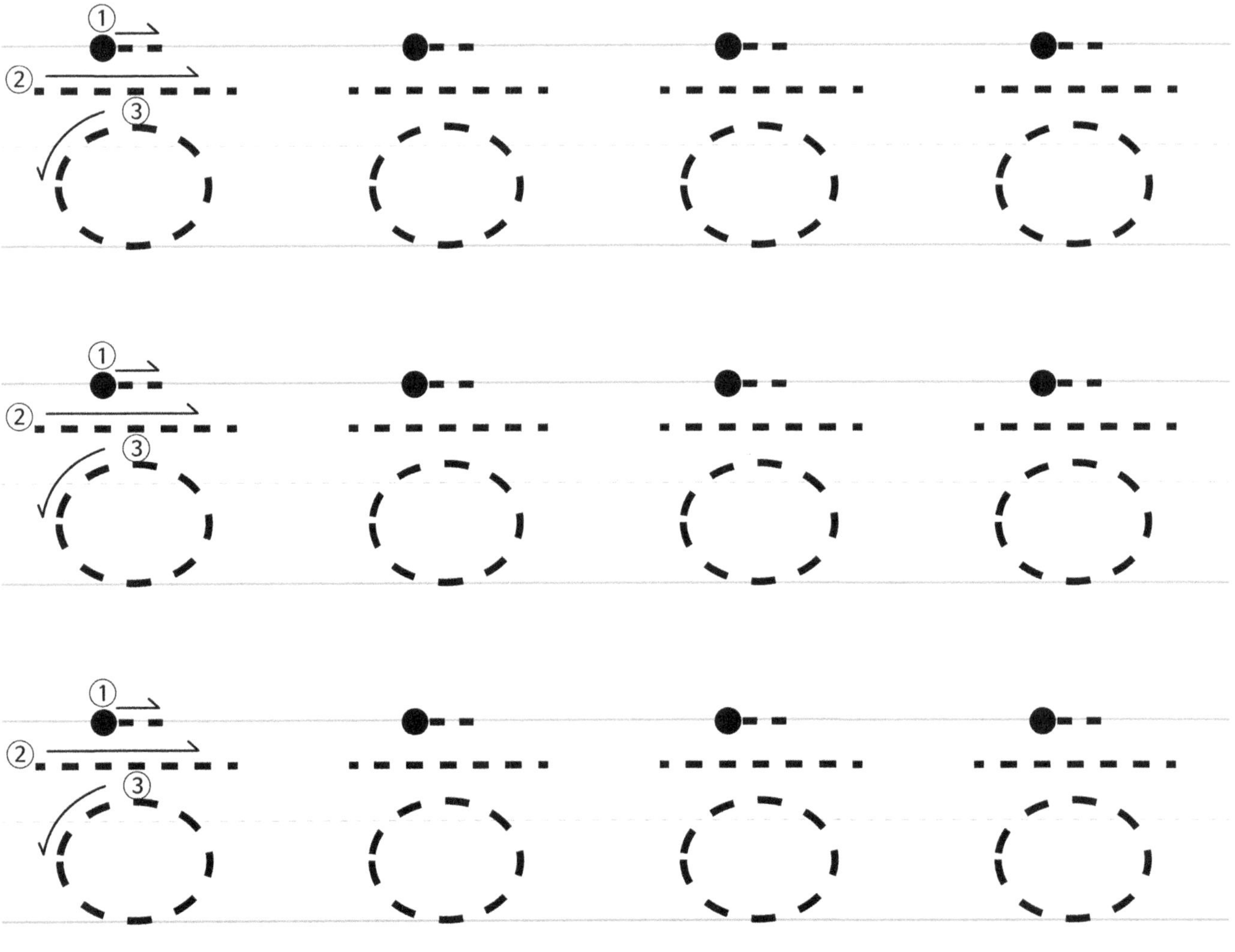

Trace it! Start at the dot! Write it!

Trace the letter. Trace the word.

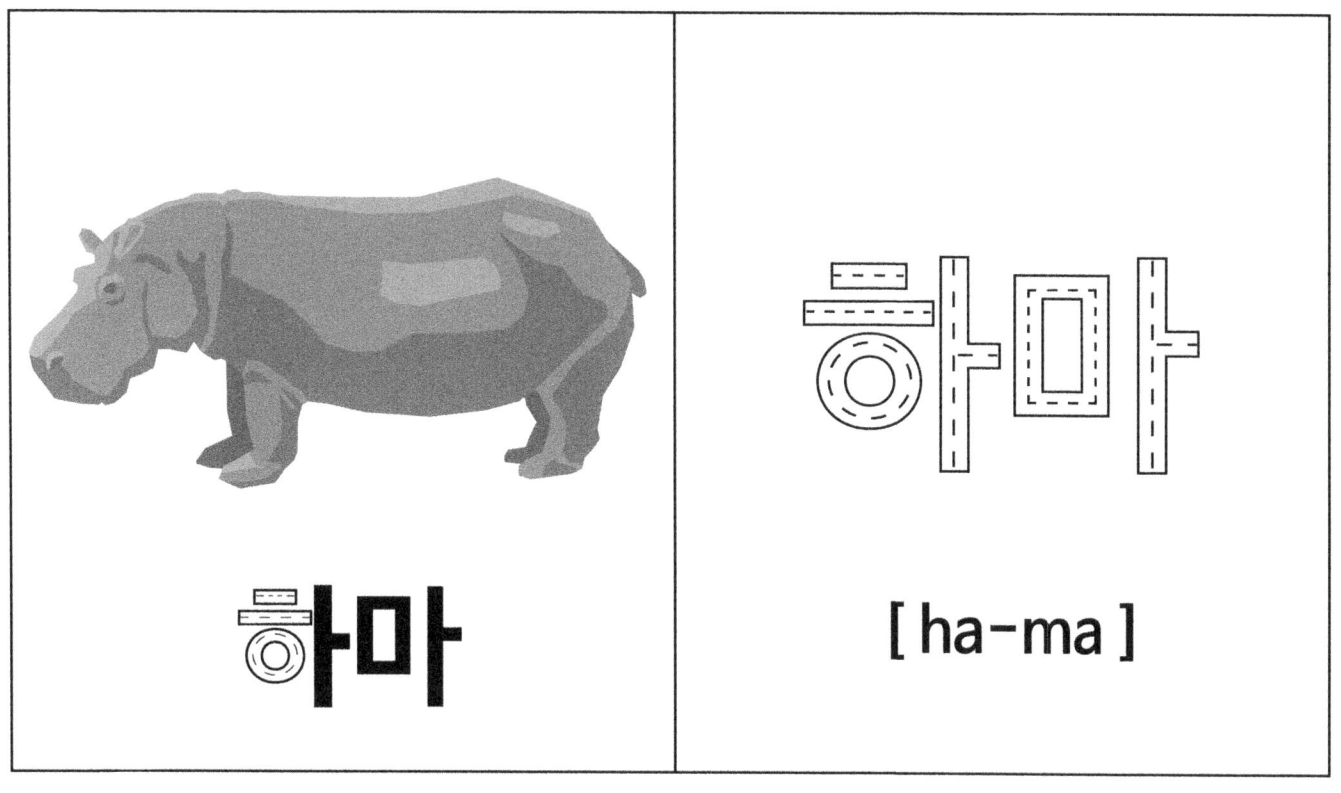

[ha-ma]

UNIT 2
쌍자음
Double Consonants

Note: In this unit, we will learn how to write the 5 double consonants.

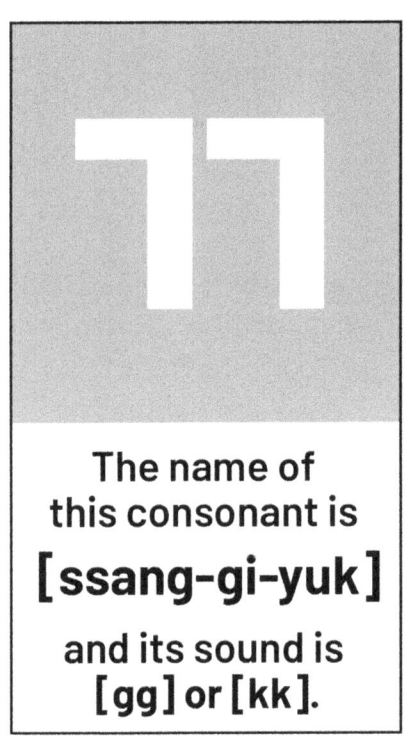

The name of this consonant is [ssang-gi-yuk]

and its sound is [gg] or [kk].

ㄲ is for 까마귀
[kka-ma-gwee]
crow

Start on the dot. Trace the dotted line. Use the arrow as a guide.

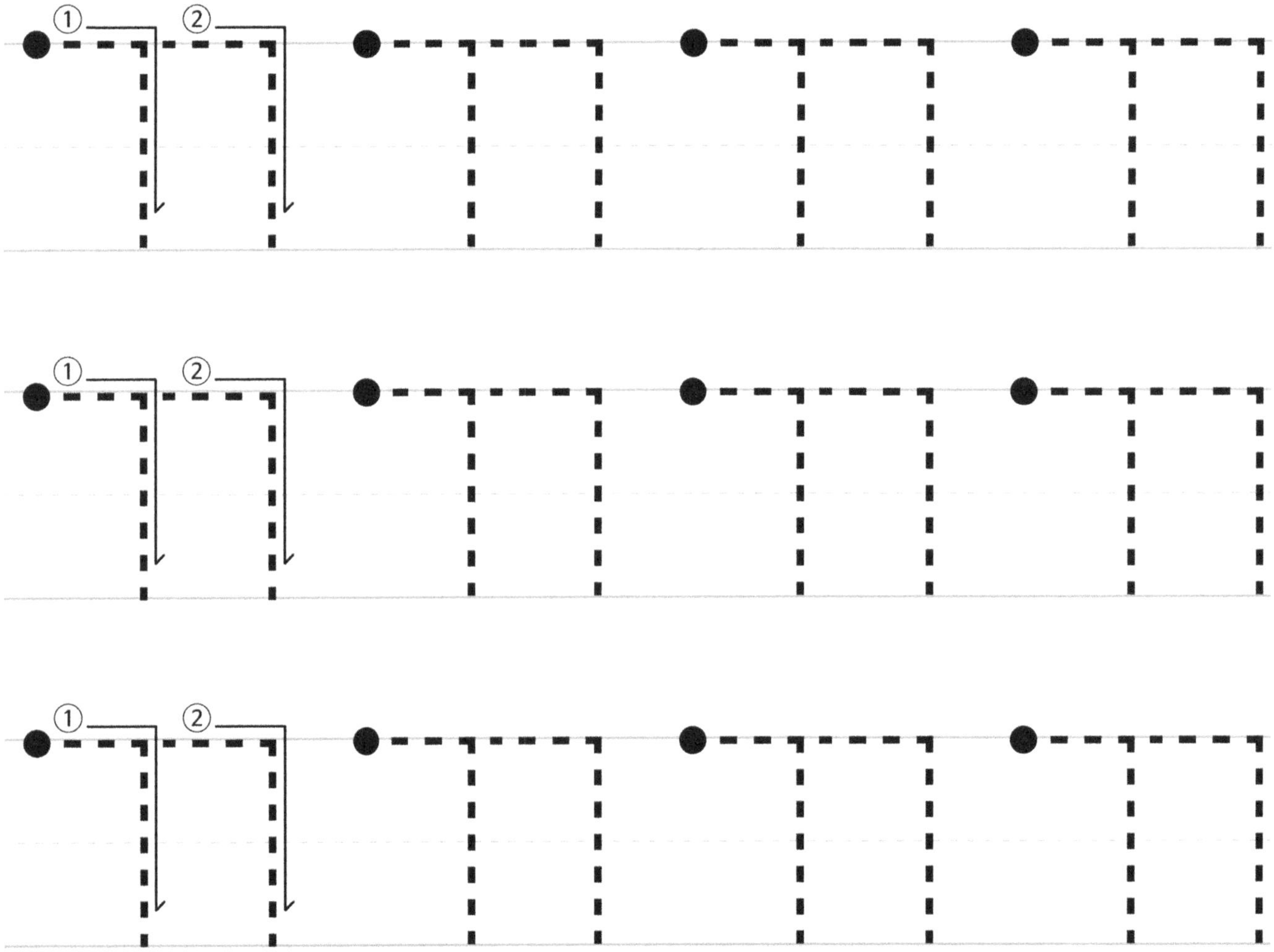

Trace it! Start at the dot! Write it!

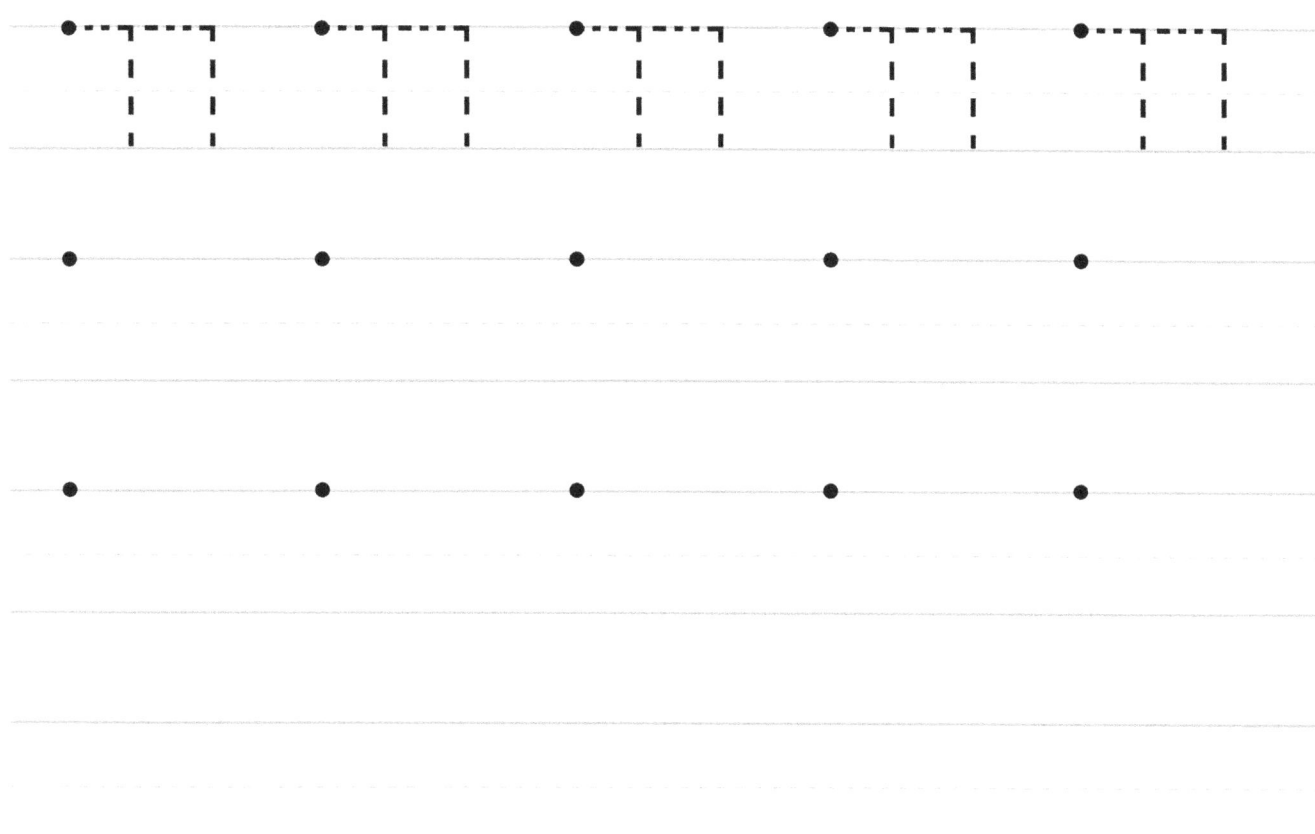

Trace the letter. Trace the word.

[kka-ma-gwee]

ㄸ is for **머리띠**
[muh-ree-ddi]
headband

The name of this consonant is **[ssang-dee-gut]** and its sound is **[dd]**.

Start on the dot. Trace the dotted line. Use the arrow as a guide.

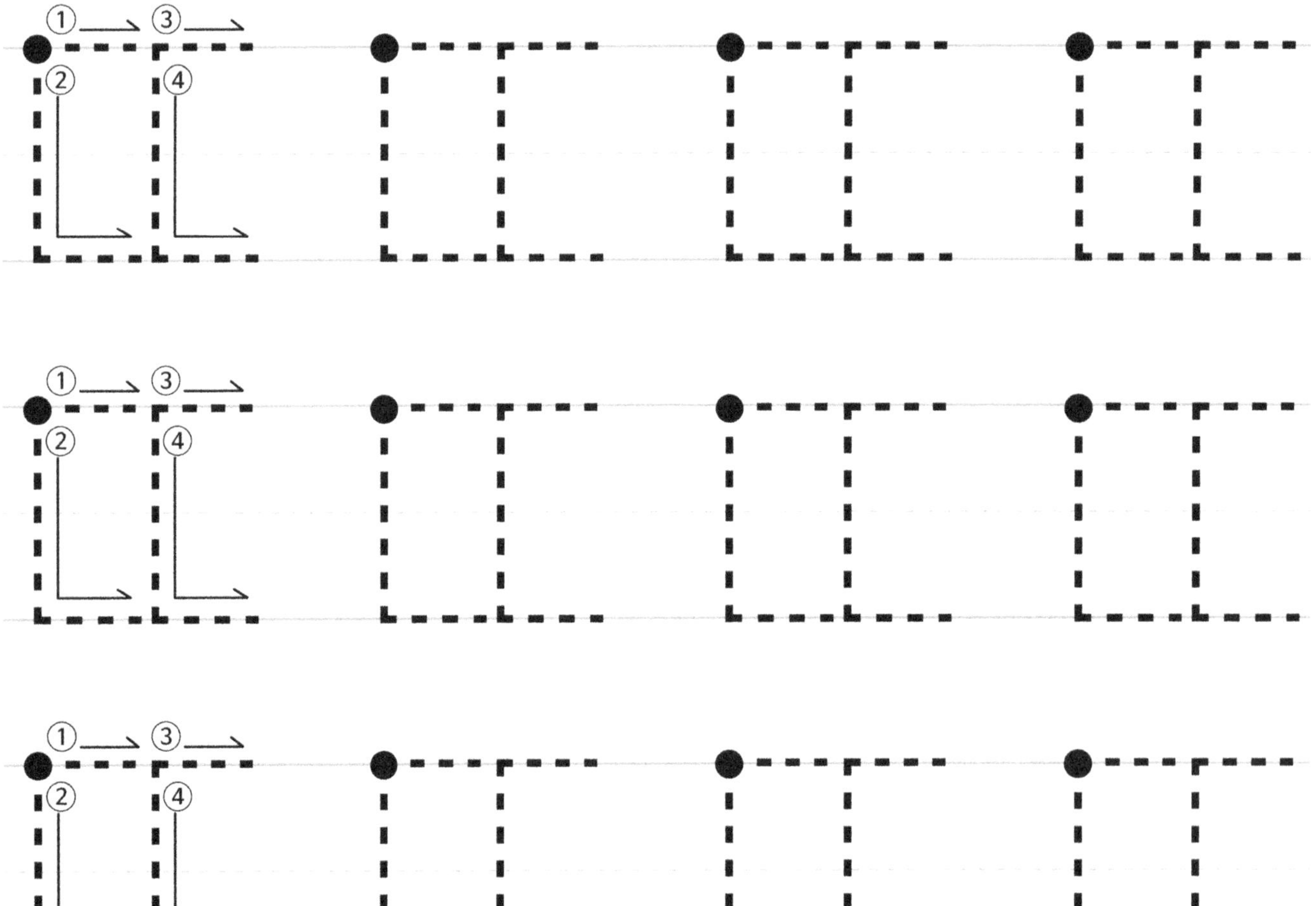

Trace it! Start at the dot! Write it!

ㄸ ㄸ ㄸ ㄸ ㄸ

Trace the letter. Trace the word.

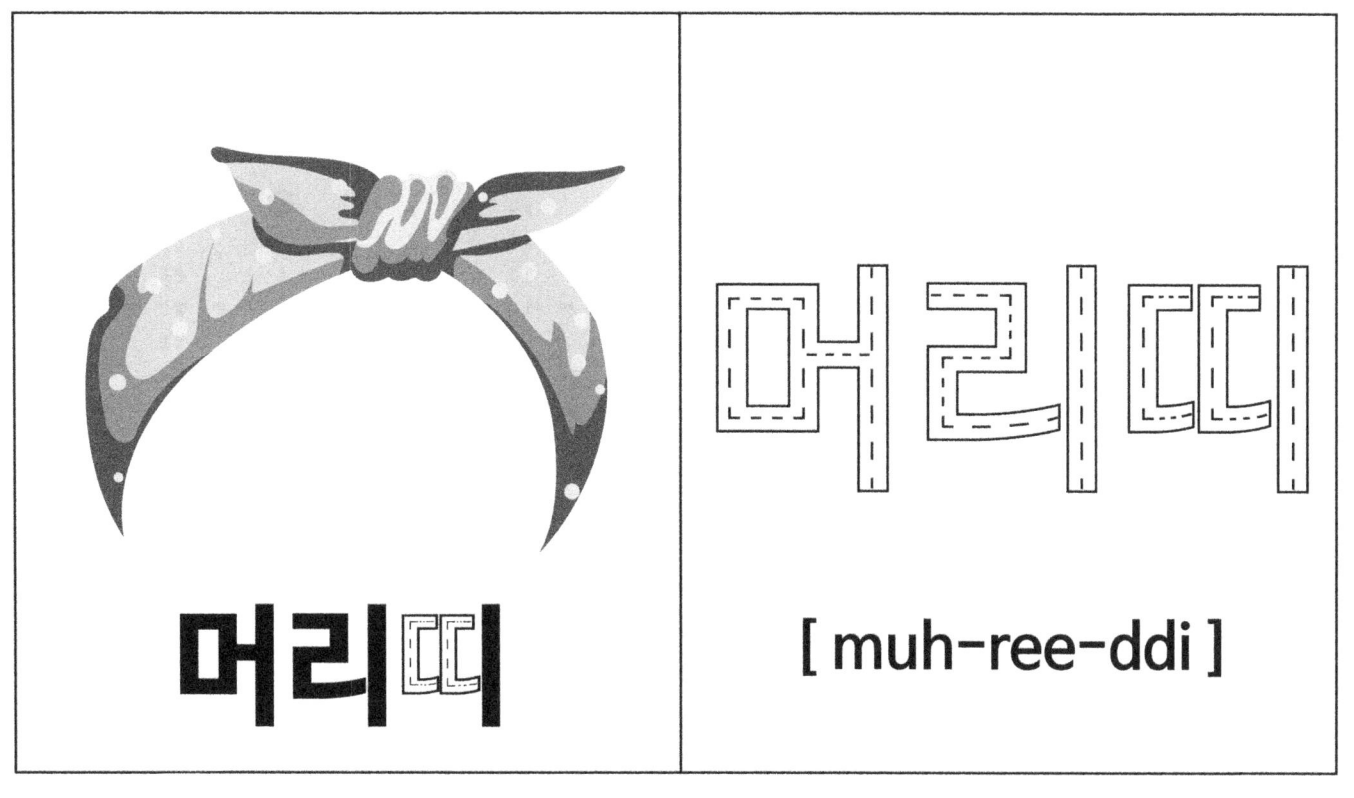

머리띠

[muh-ree-ddi]

The name of this consonant is [ssang-bee-eup] and its sound is [bb].

ㅃ is for 빵
[bbang]
bread

Start on the dot. Trace the dotted line. Use the arrow as a guide.

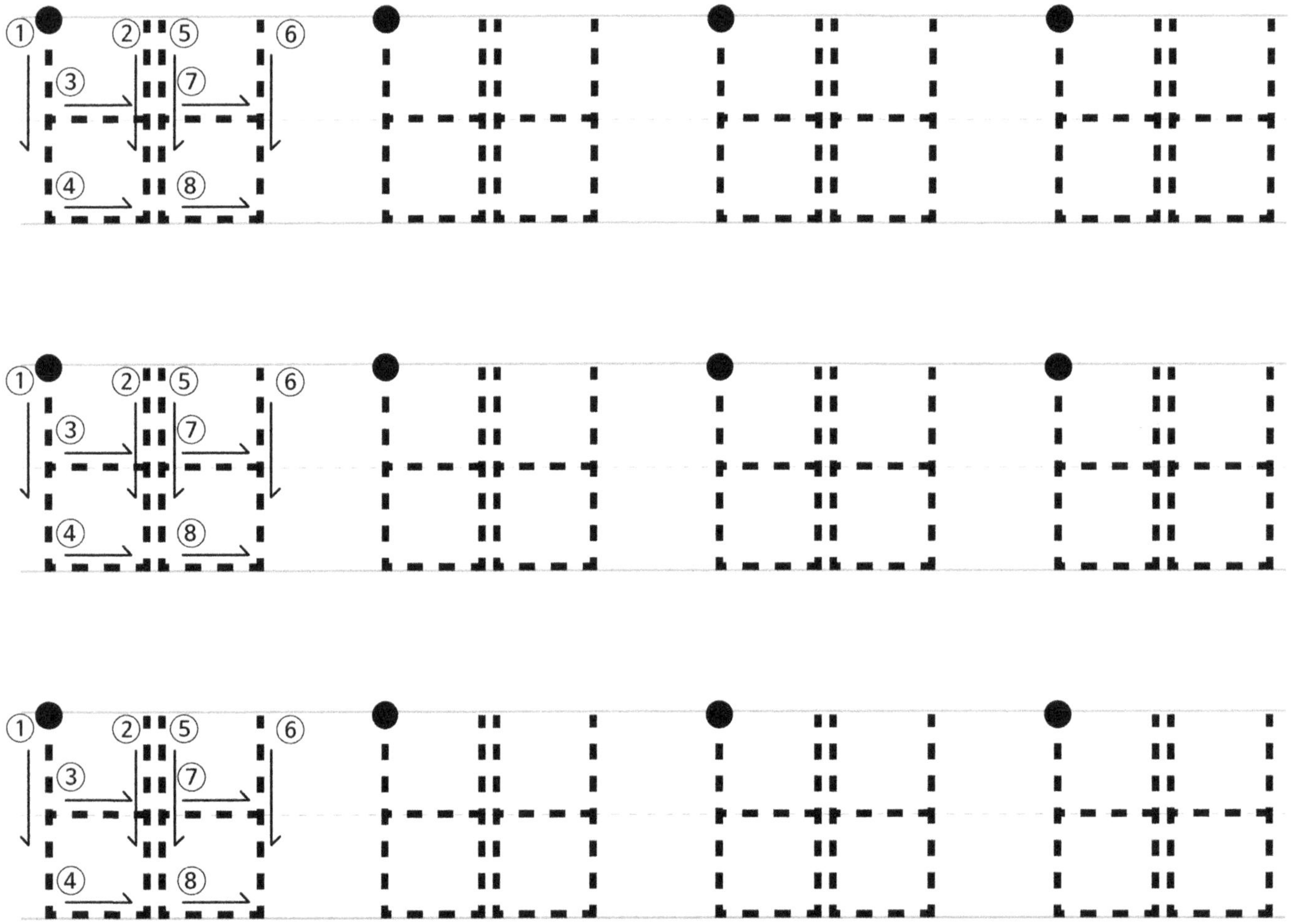

Trace it! Start at the dot! Write it!

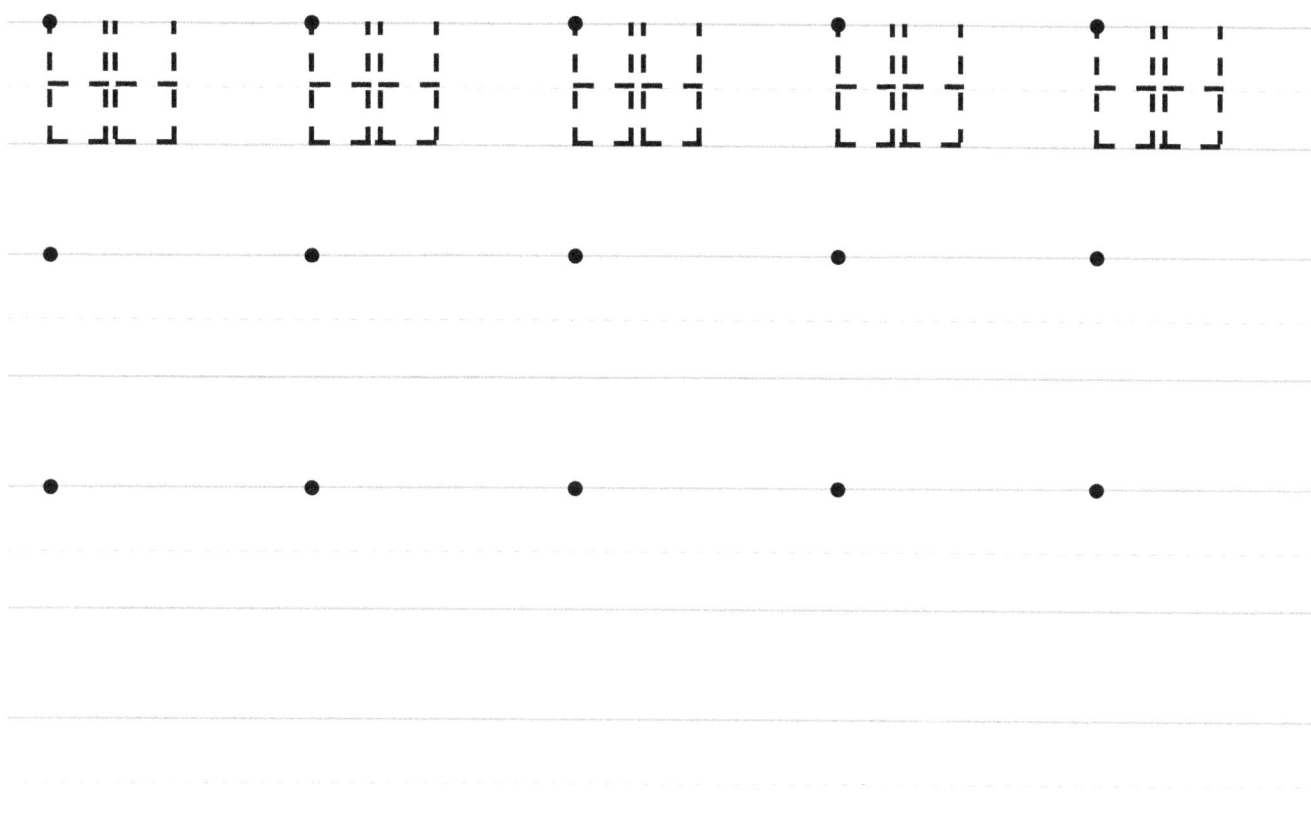

Trace the letter. Trace the word.

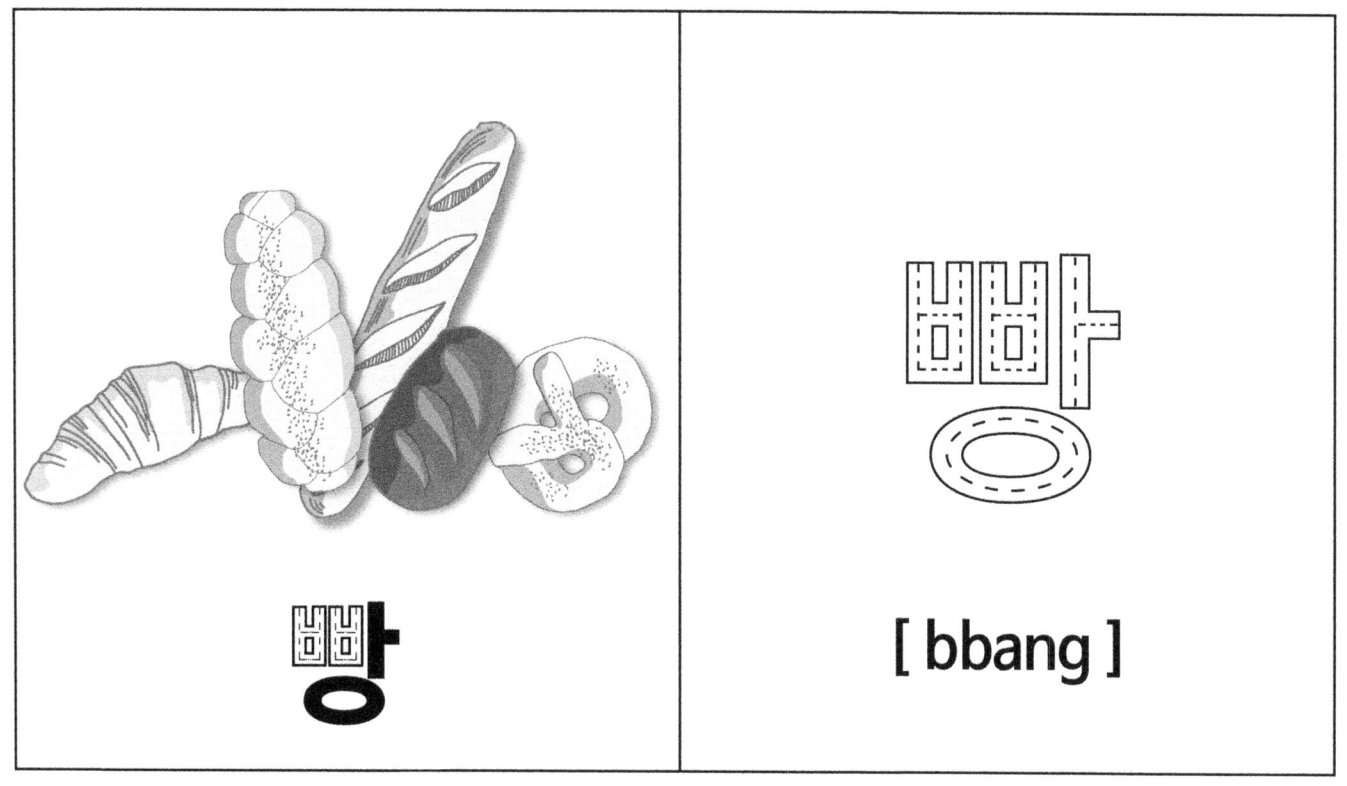

[bbang]

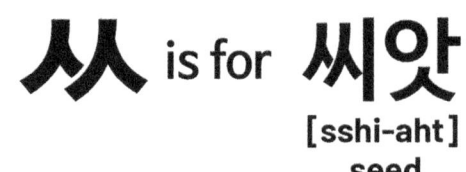 is for 씨앗
[sshi-aht]
seed

The name of this consonant is **[ssang-shee-ot]** and its sound is **[ss]**.

Start on the dot. Trace the dotted line. Use the arrow as a guide.

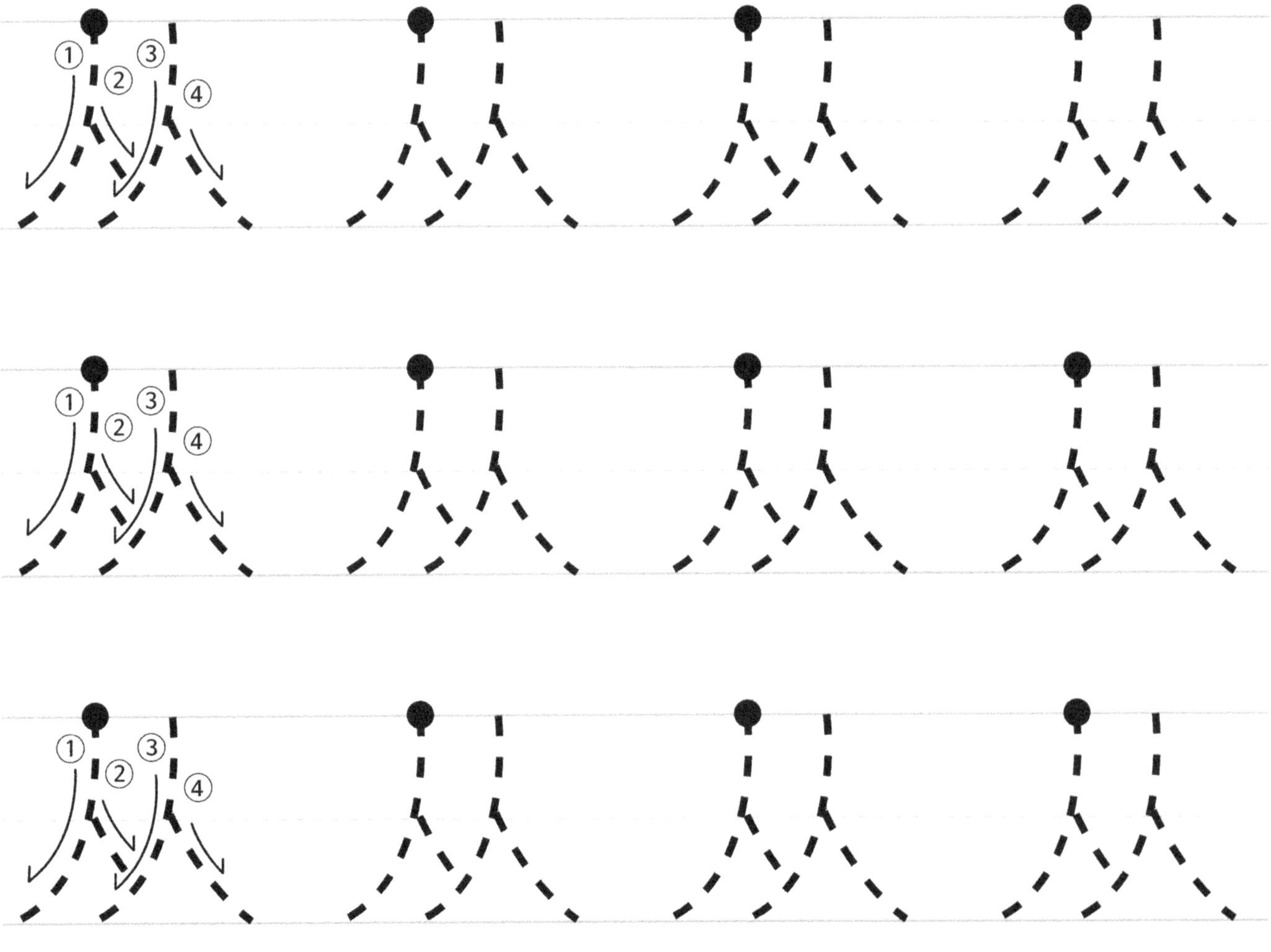

Trace it! Start at the dot! Write it!

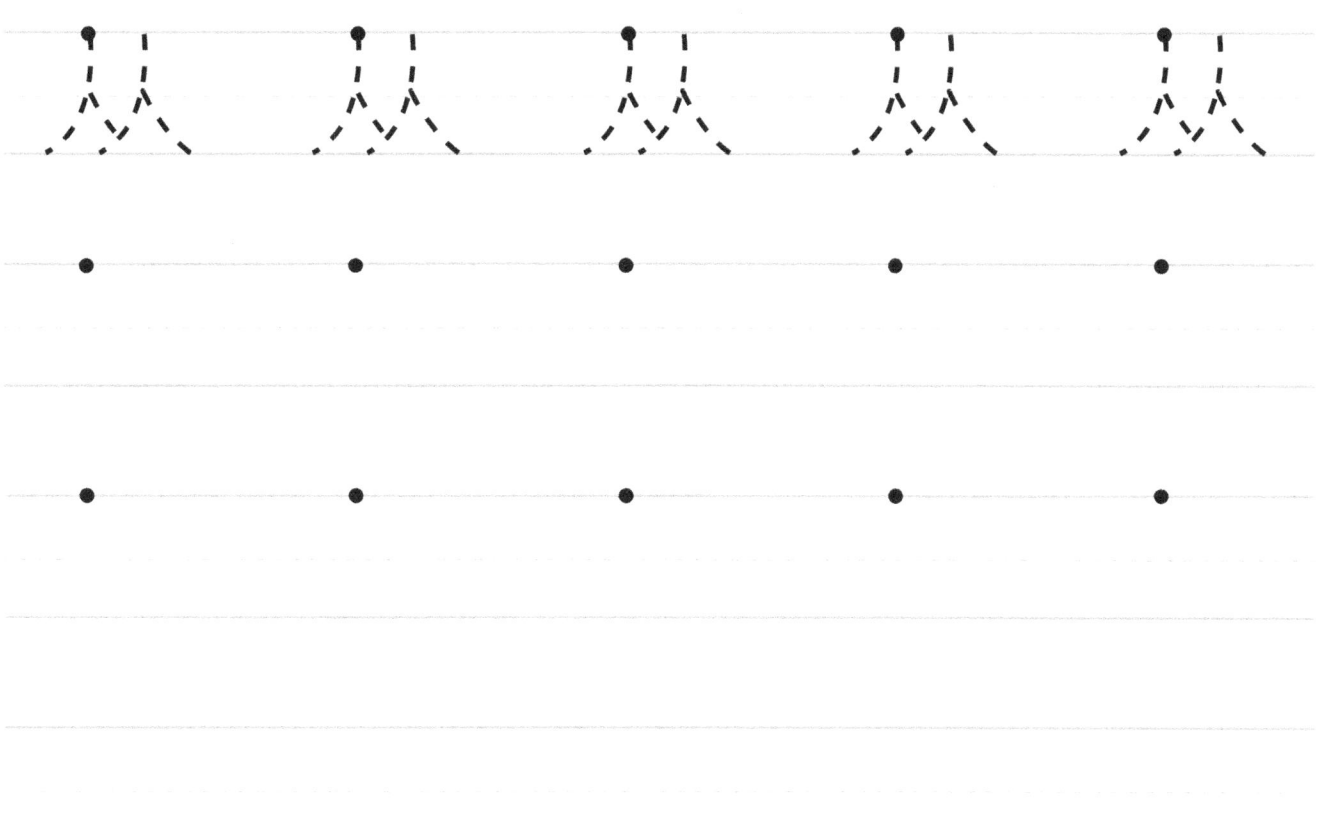

Trace the letter. Trace the word.

씨앗

[sshi-aht]

The name of this consonant is **[ssang-jee-eut]** and its sound is **[jj]**.

ㅉ is for **찌개**
[jji-gae]
stew

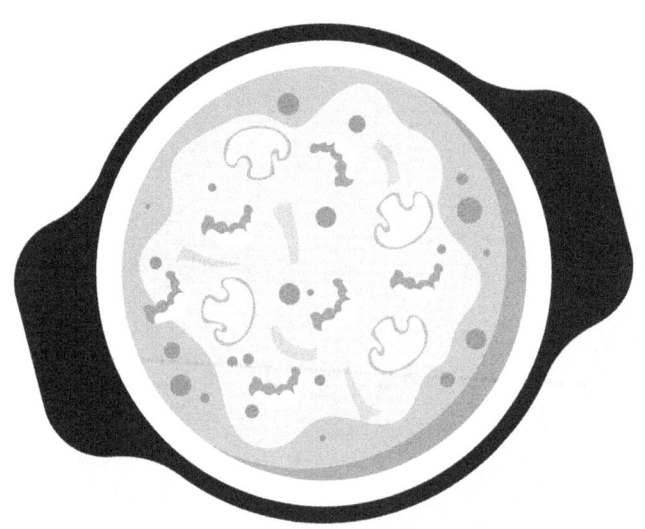

Start on the dot. Trace the dotted line. Use the arrow as a guide.

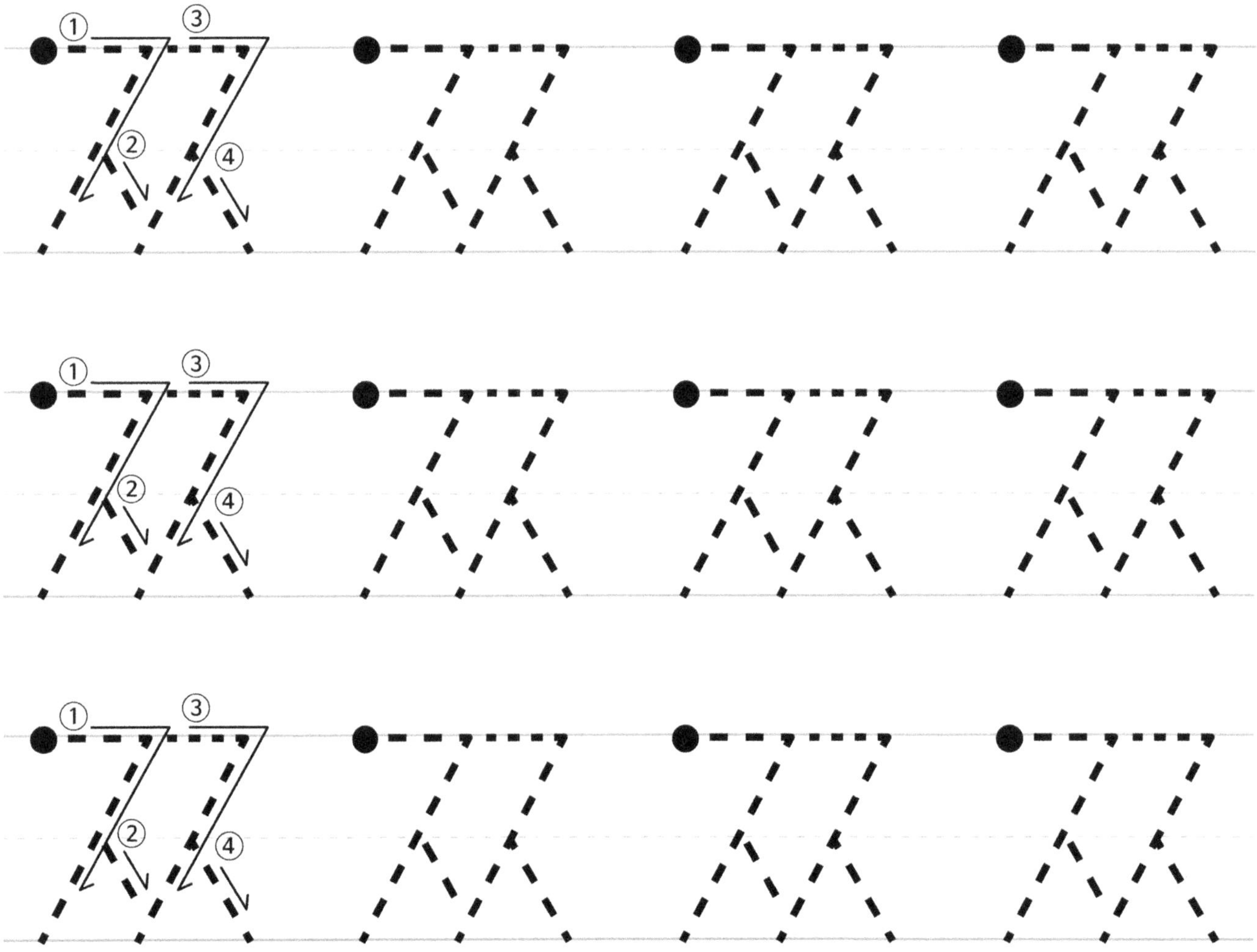

Trace it! Start at the dot! Write it!

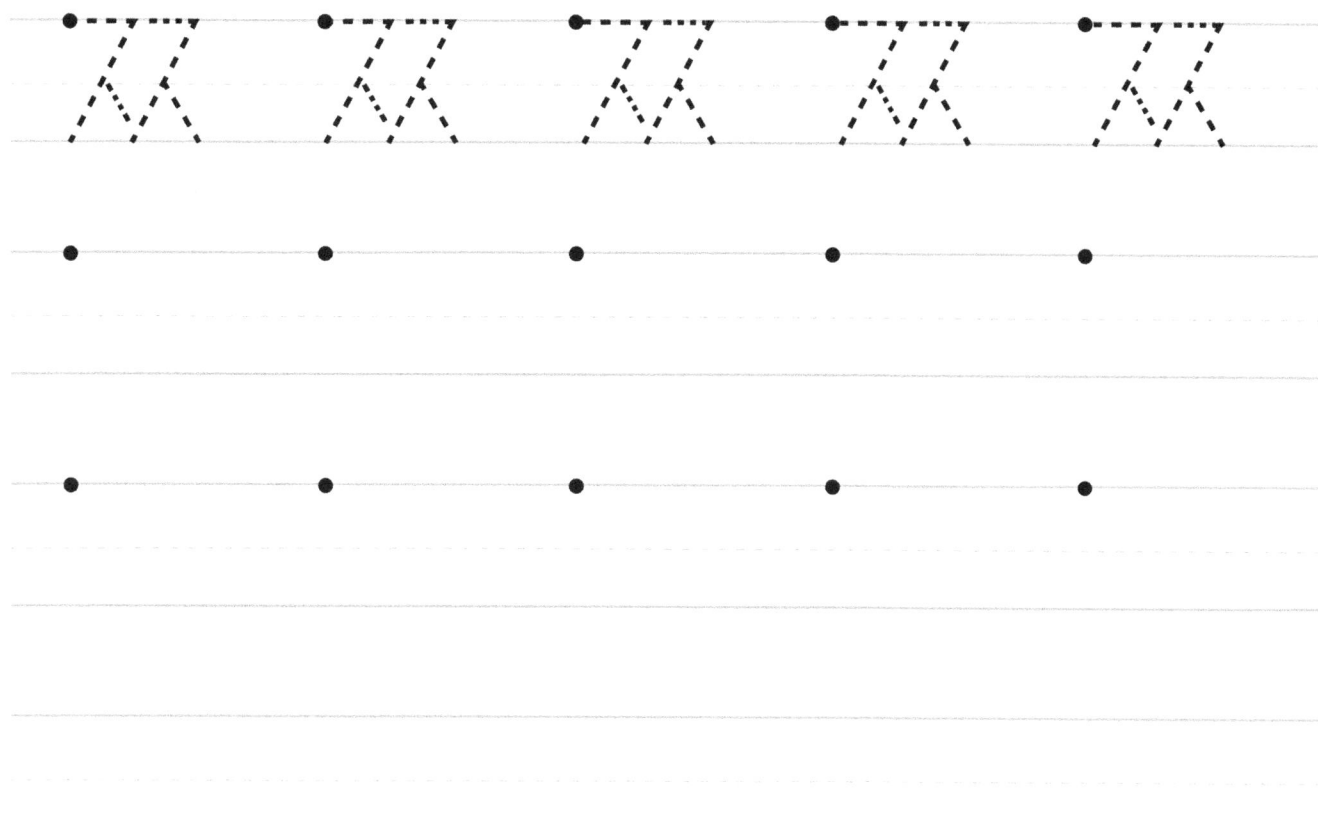

Trace the letter. Trace the word.

찌개

[jji-gae]

UNIT 3

모음
Vowels

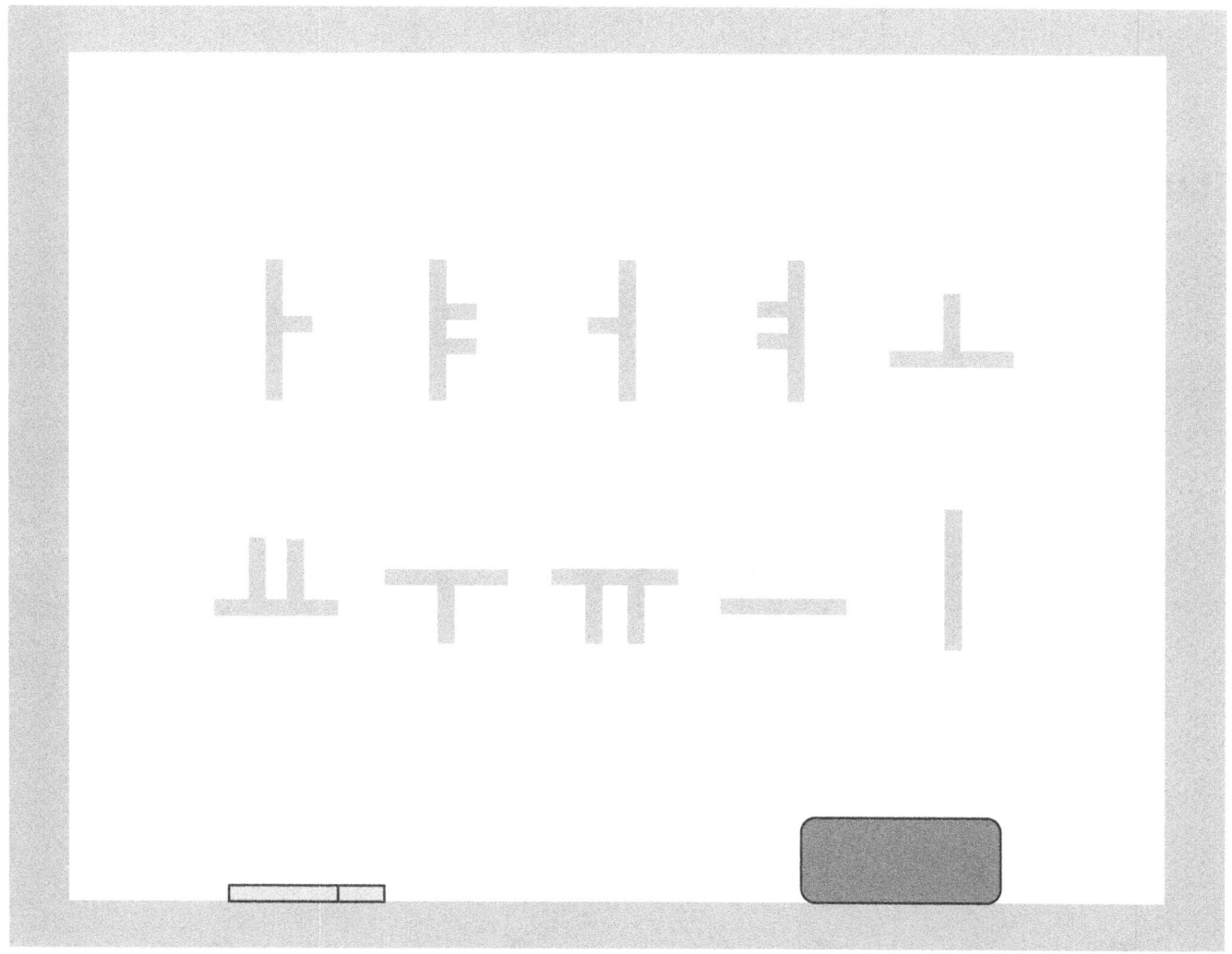

Note: In this unit, we will learn how to write the 10 basic vowels.

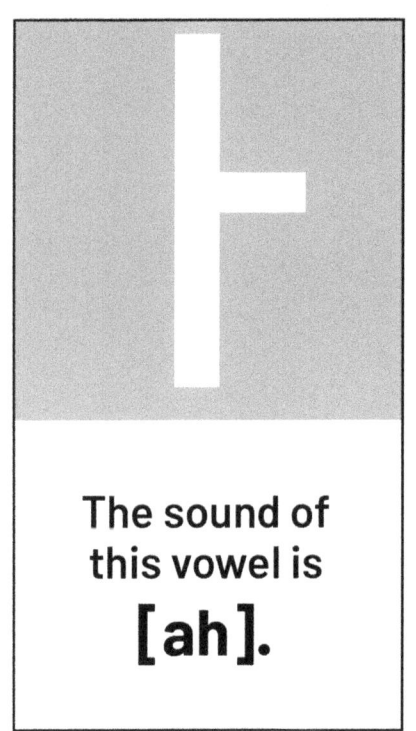

The sound of this vowel is **[ah]**.

ㅏ is for 아빠
[ah-bba]
dad

Start on the dot. Trace the dotted line. Use the arrow as a guide.

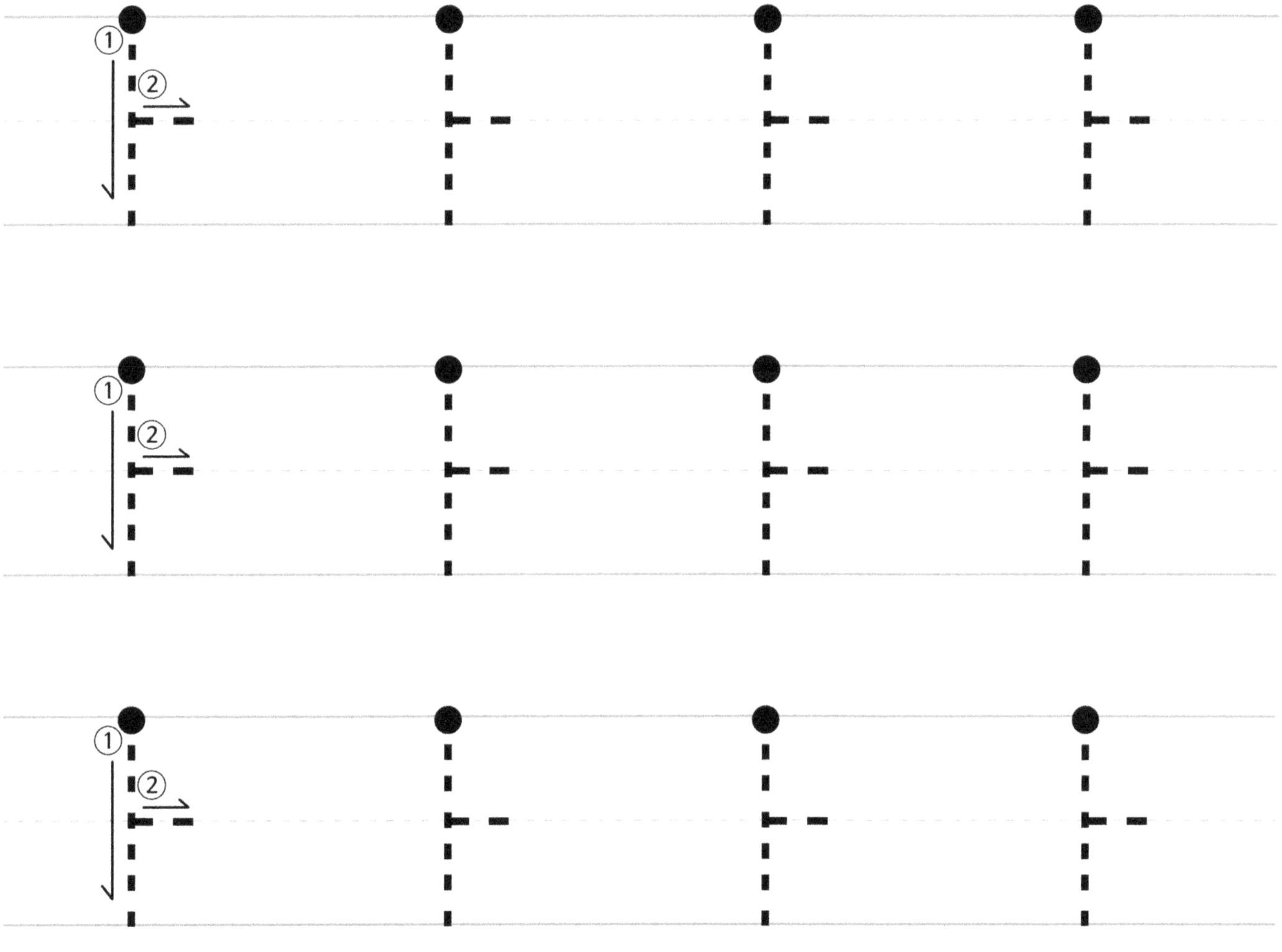

Trace it! Start at the dot! Write it!

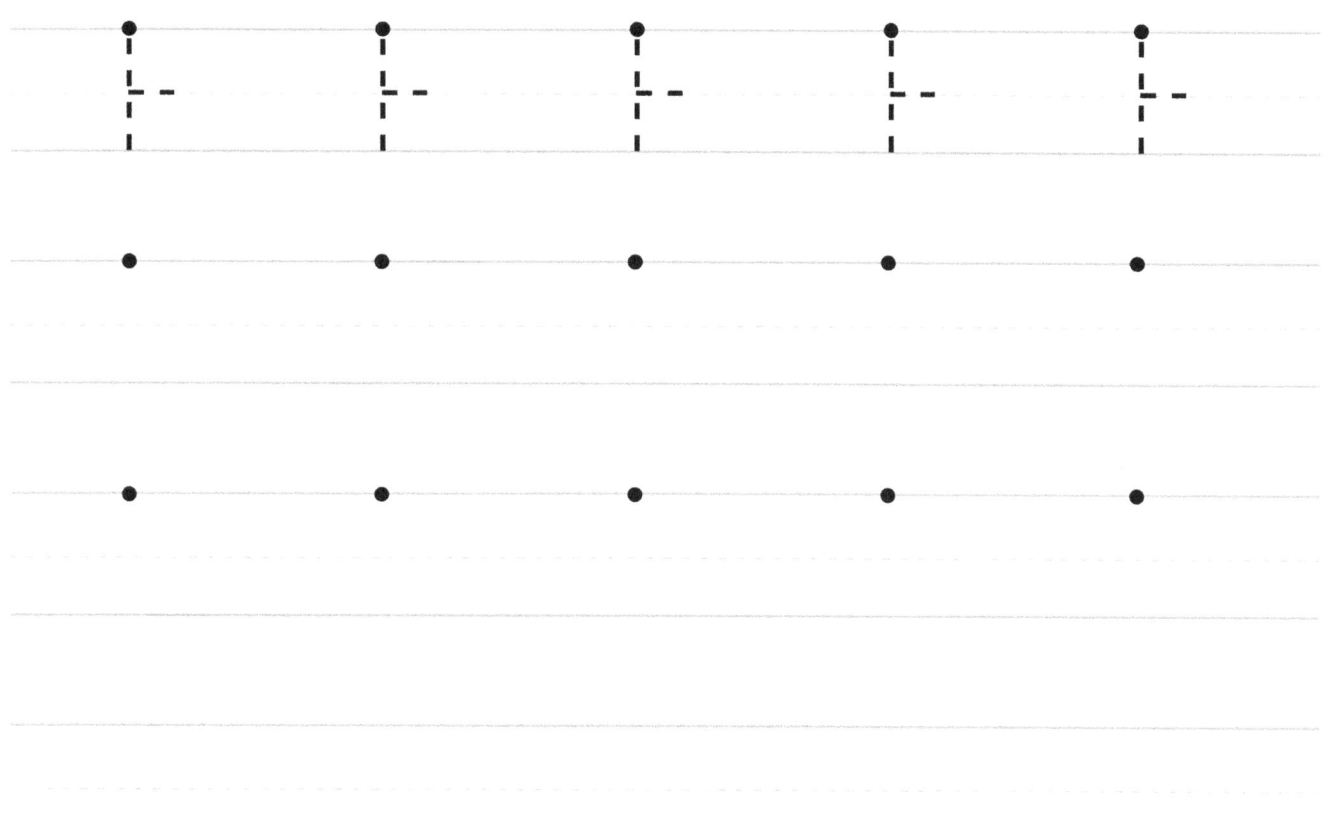

Trace the letter. Trace the word.

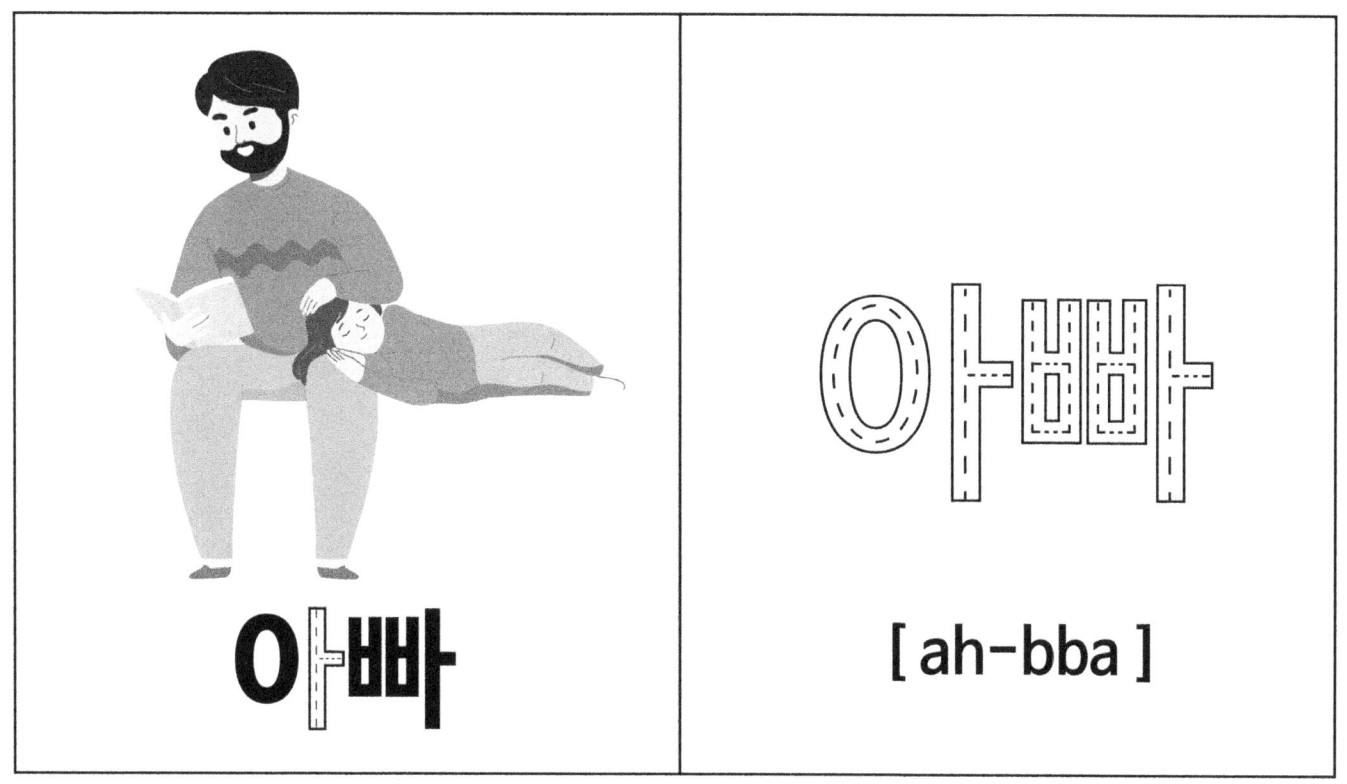

[ah-bba]

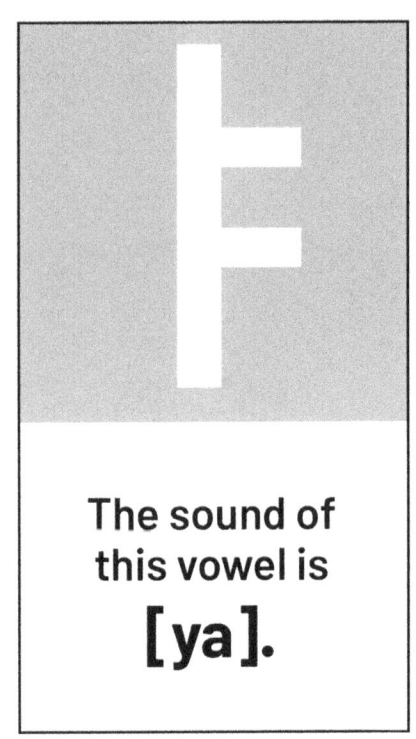

The sound of this vowel is **[ya]**.

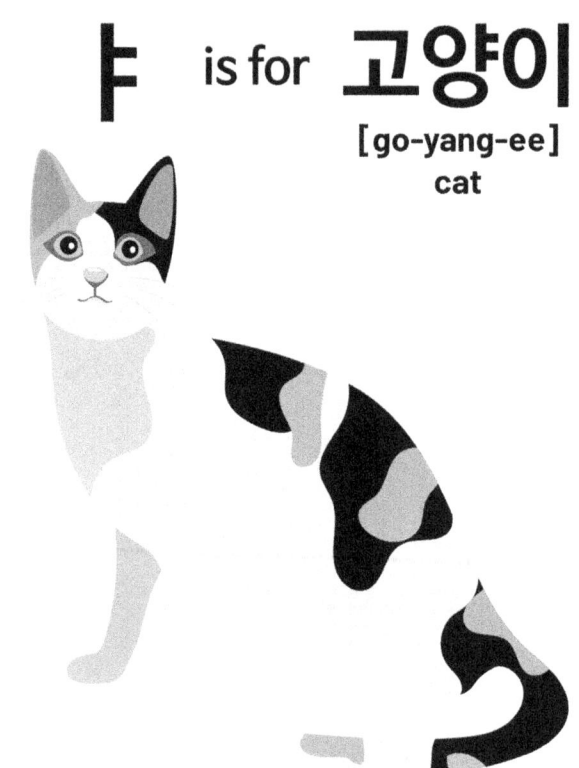

ㅑ is for 고양이
[go-yang-ee]
cat

Start on the dot. Trace the dotted line. Use the arrow as a guide.

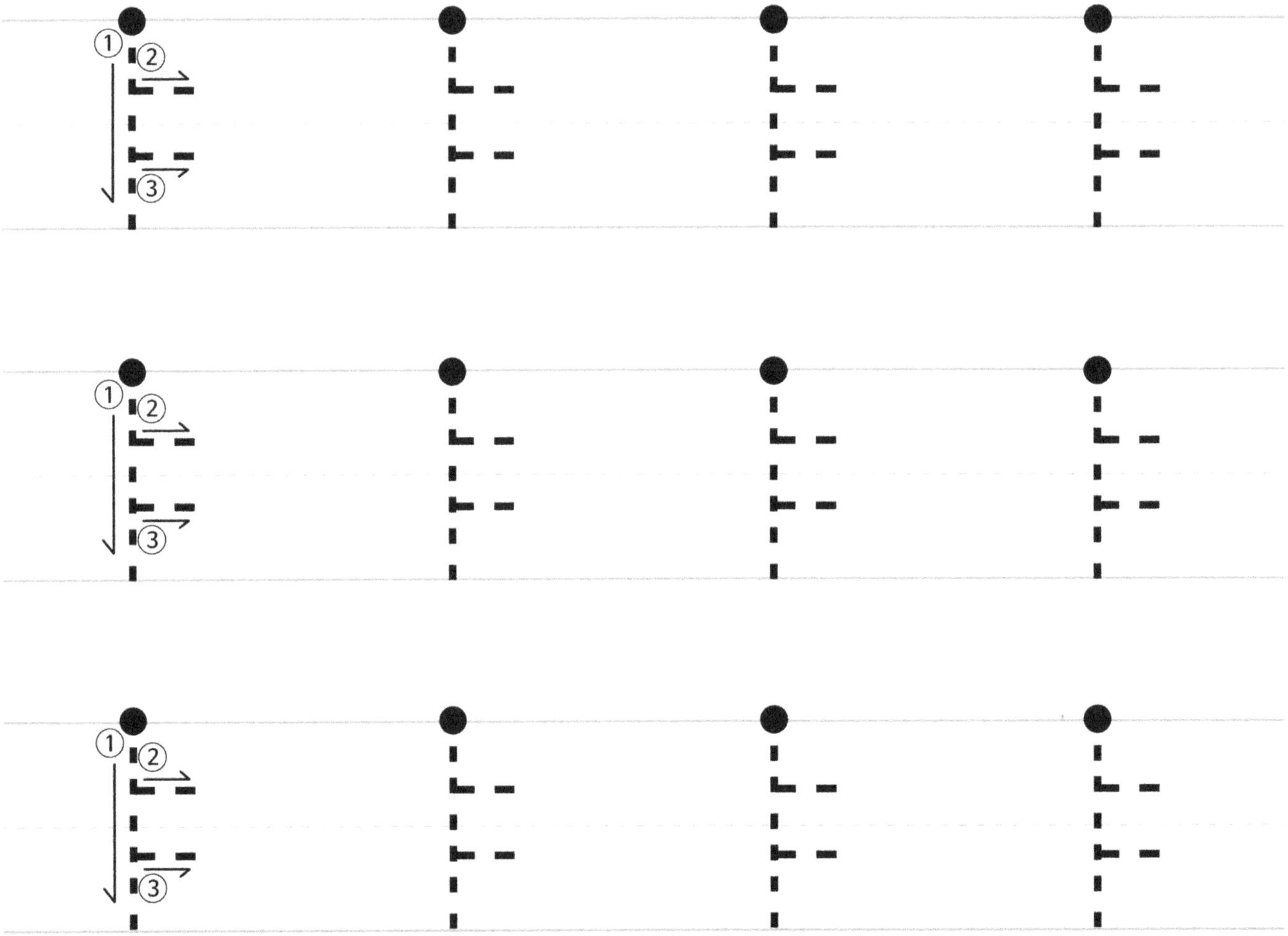

Trace it! Start at the dot! Write it!

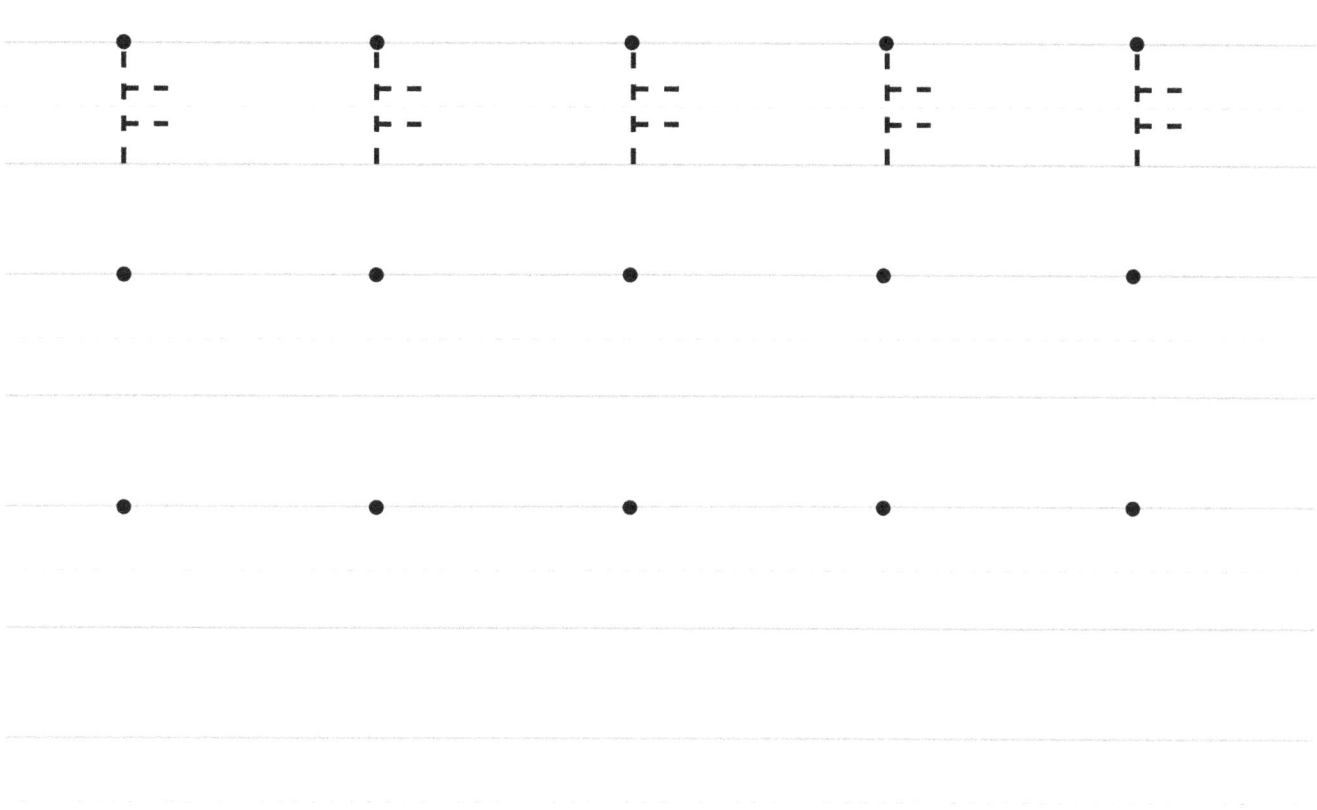

Trace the letter. Trace the word.

고양이

[go-yang-ee]

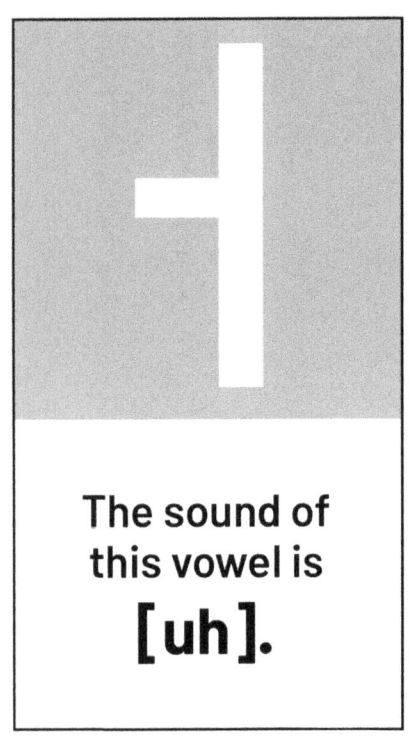

ㅓ is for 엄마
[um-ma]
mom

The sound of this vowel is [uh].

Start on the dot. Trace the dotted line. Use the arrow as a guide.

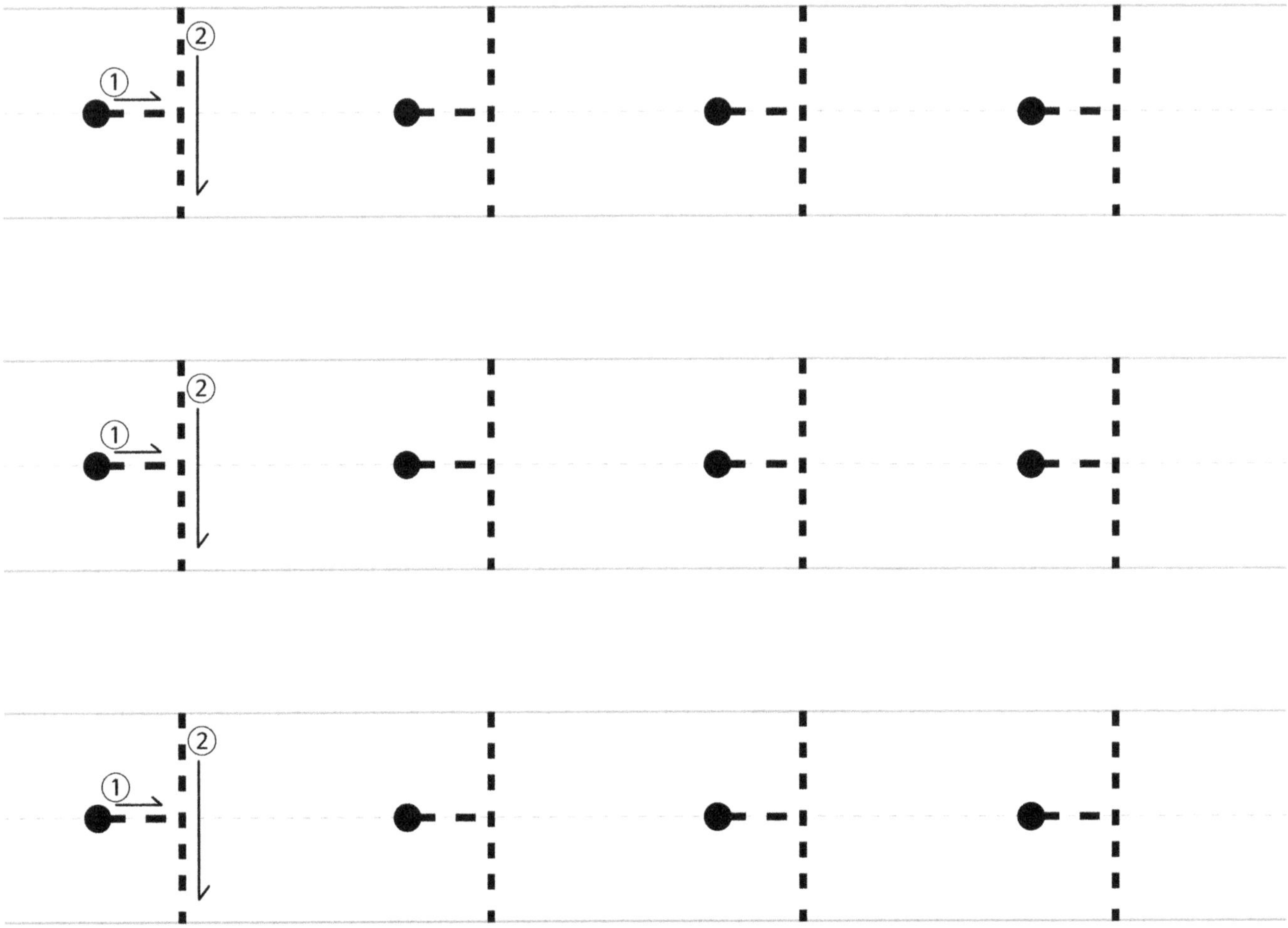

Trace it! Start at the dot! Write it!

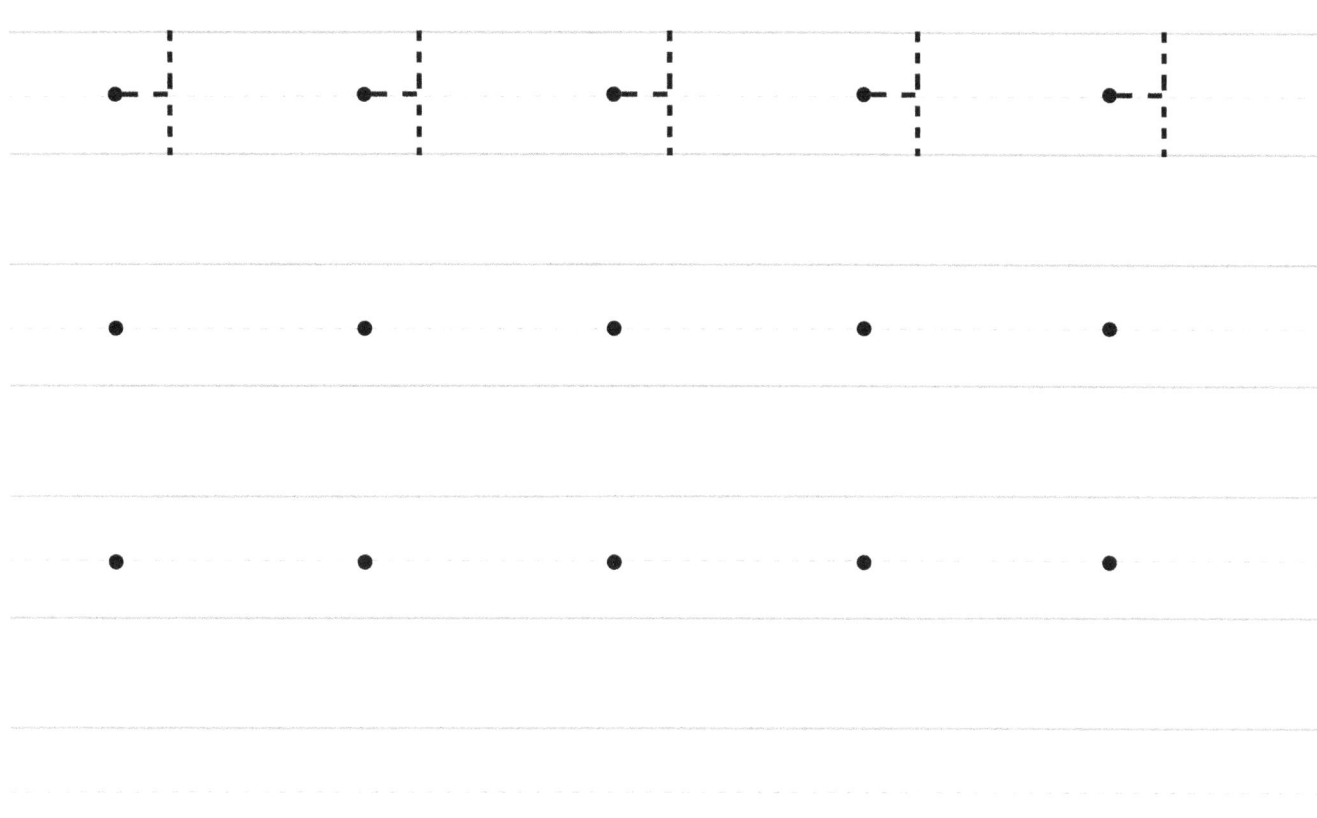

Trace the letter. Trace the word.

[um-ma]

ㅕ is for 안경
[ahn-kyung]
glasses

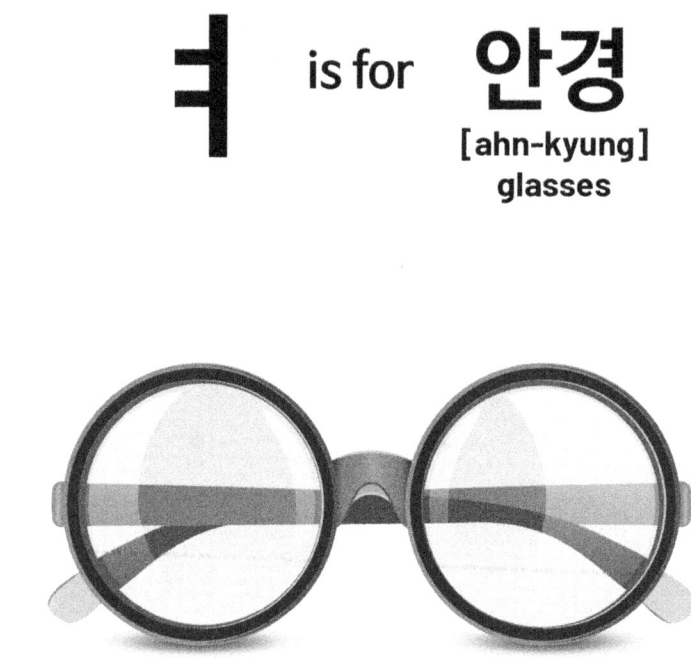

The sound of this vowel is **[yuh]**.

Start on the dot. Trace the dotted line. Use the arrow as a guide.

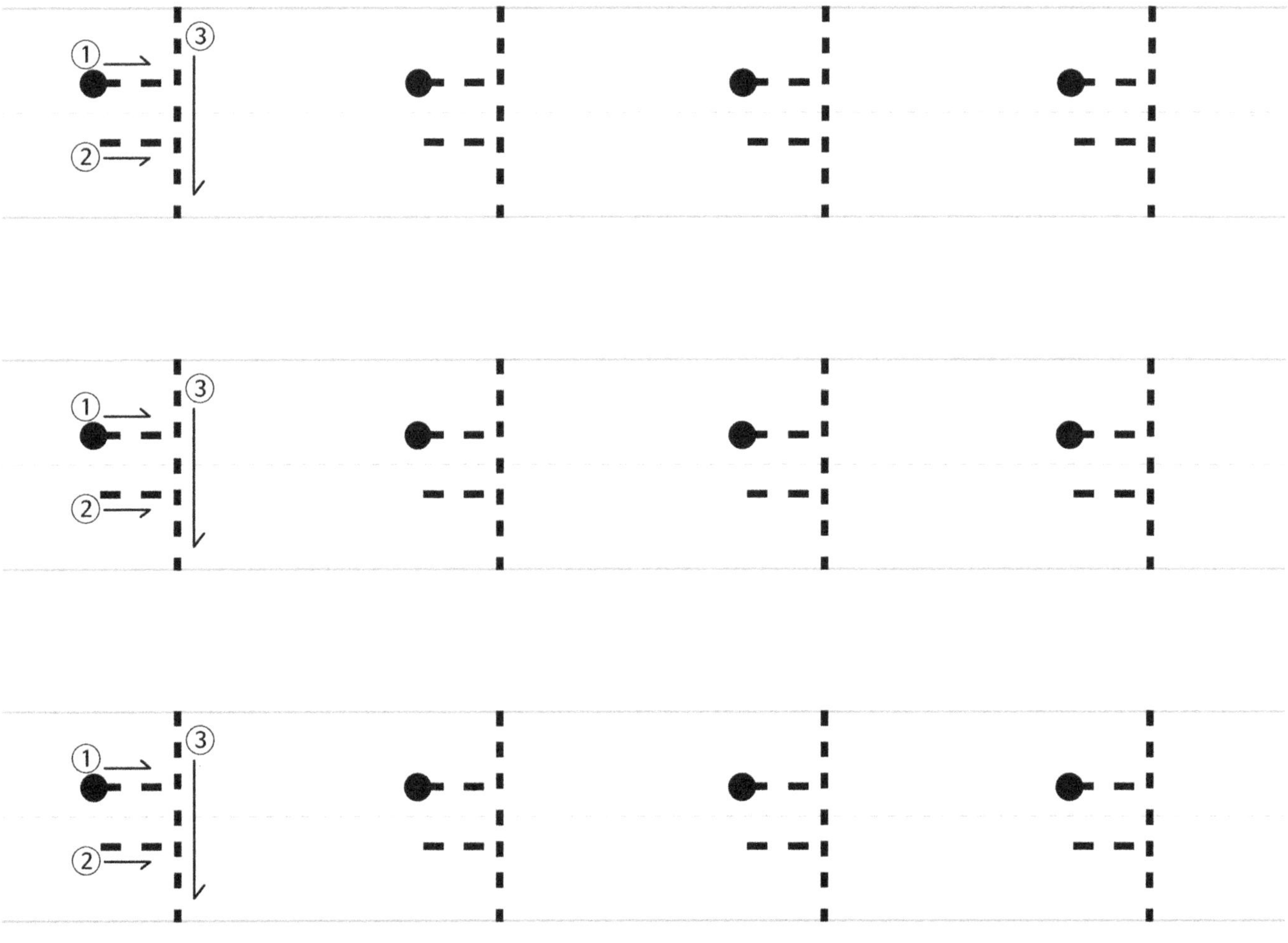

Trace it! Start at the dot! Write it!

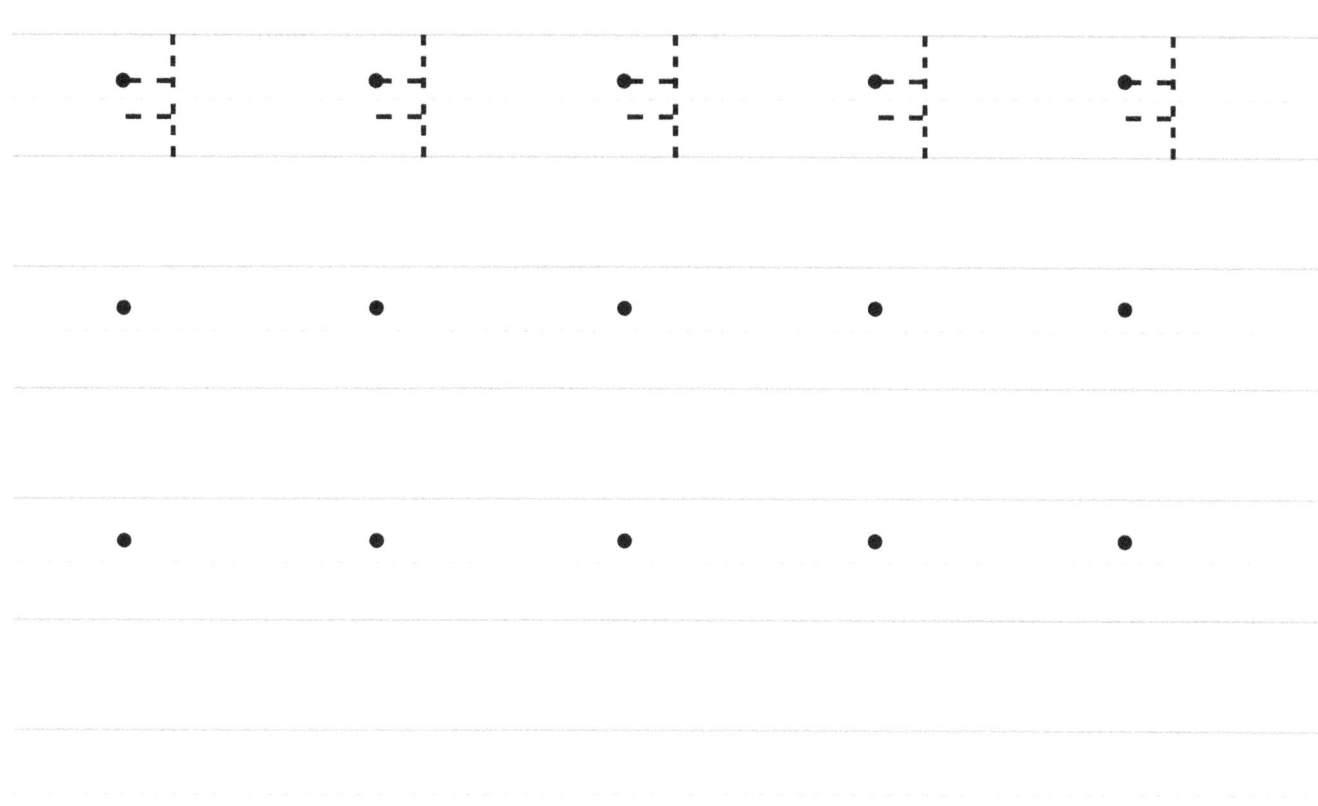

Trace the letter. Trace the word.

안경

[ahn-kyung]

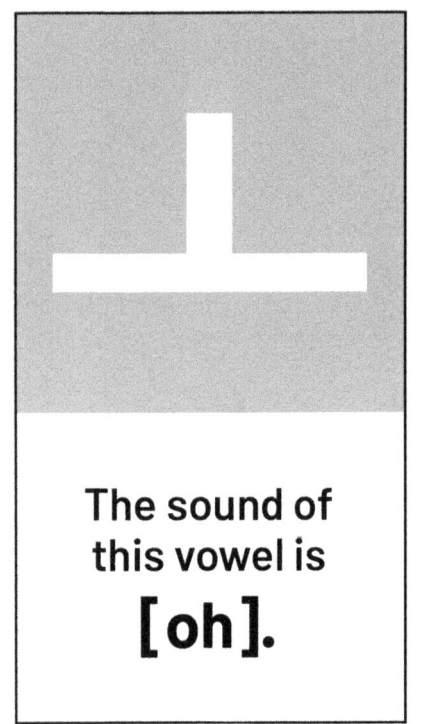

ㅗ is for 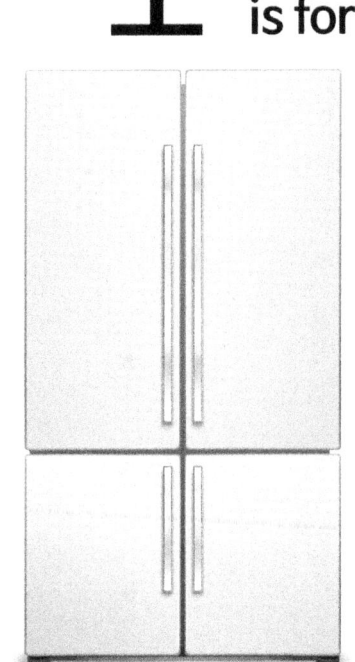 **냉장고**
[nang-jang-go]
refrigerator

The sound of this vowel is **[oh]**.

Start on the dot. Trace the dotted line. Use the arrow as a guide.

Trace it! Start at the dot! Write it!

Trace the letter. Trace the word.

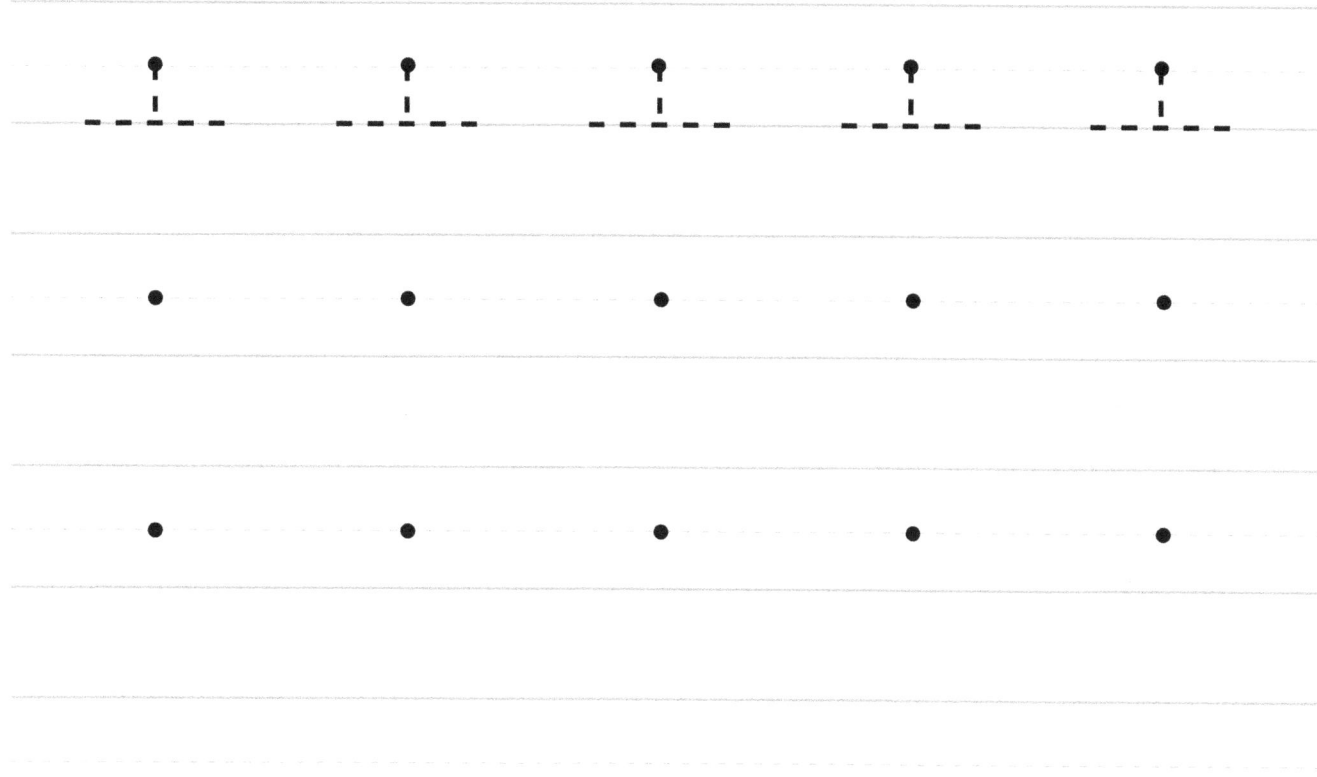

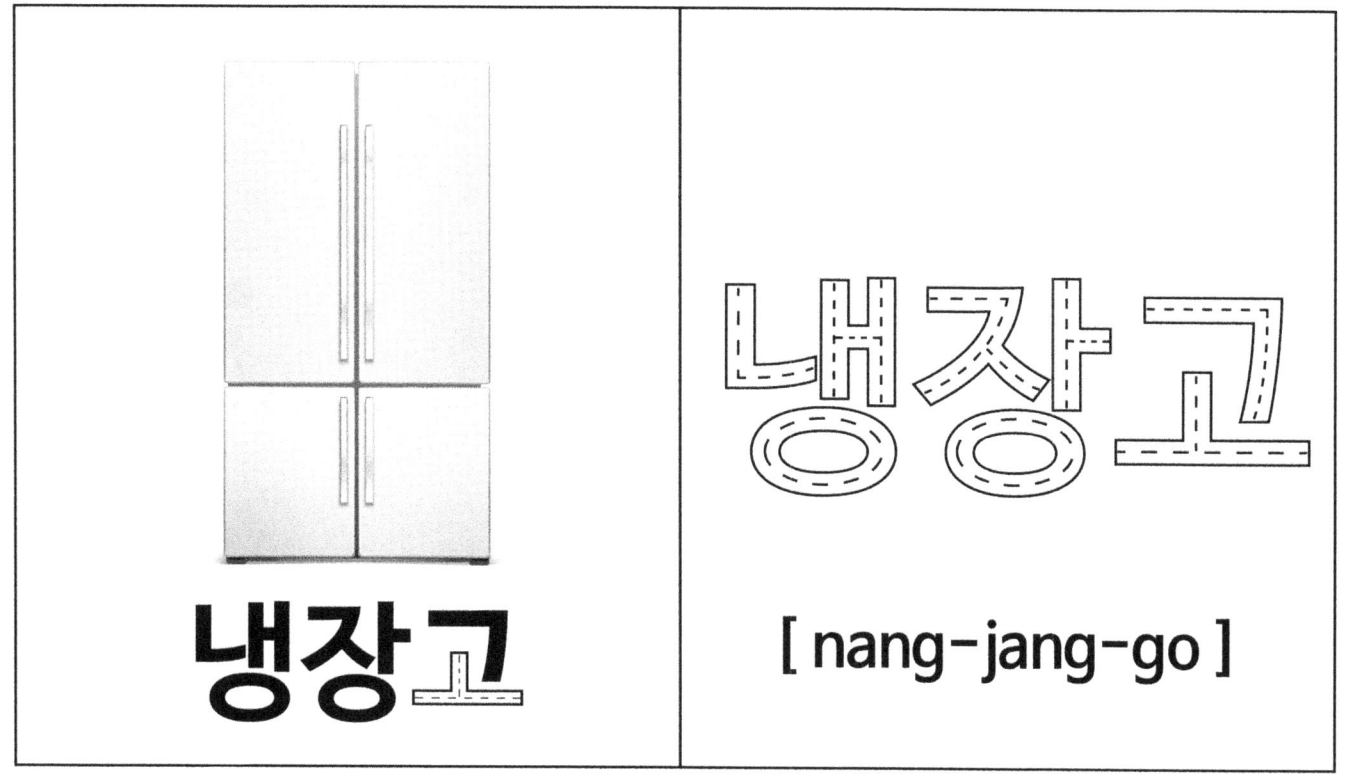

[nang-jang-go]

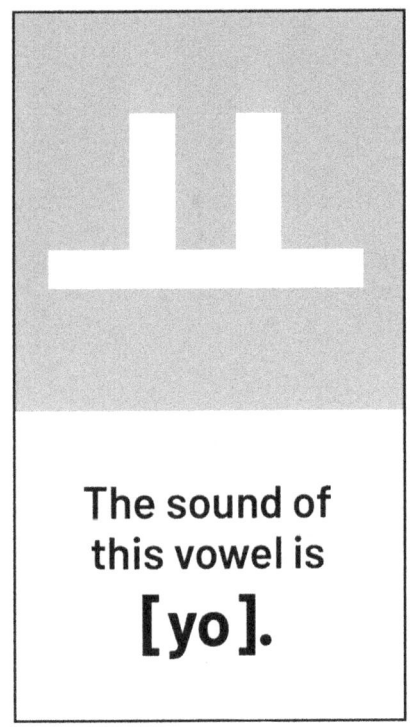

The sound of this vowel is **[yo]**.

ㅛ is for 요가
[yo-ga]
yoga

Start on the dot. Trace the dotted line. Use the arrow as a guide.

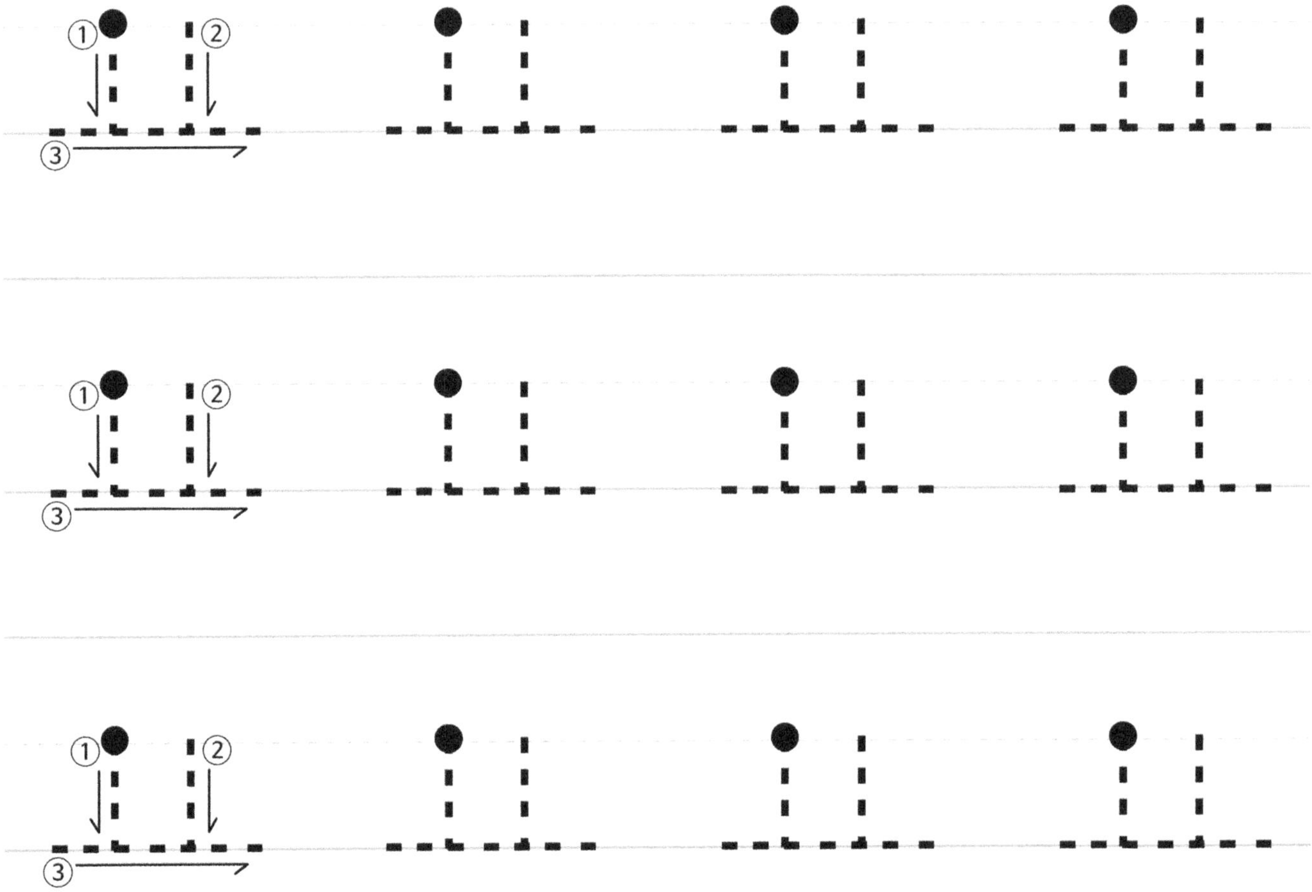

Trace it! Start at the dot! Write it!

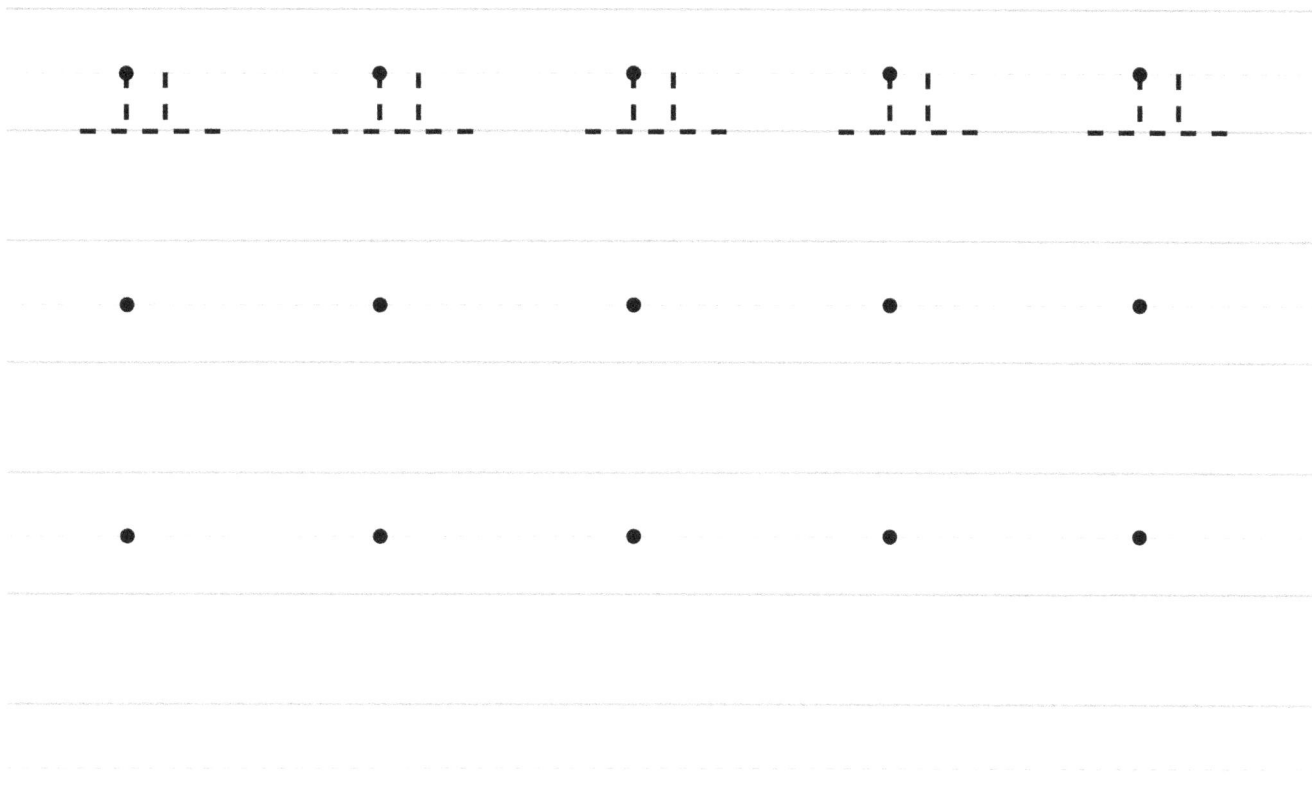

Trace the letter. Trace the word.

요가

[yoga]

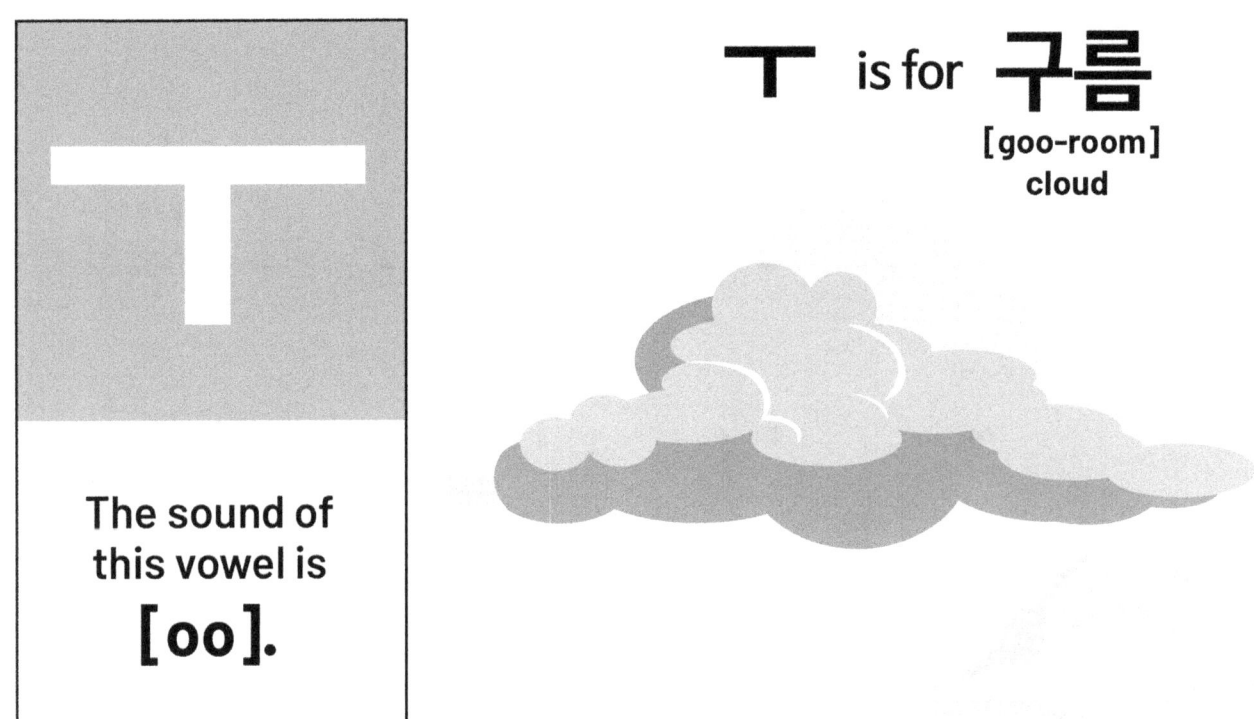

ㅜ is for 구름
[goo-room]
cloud

The sound of this vowel is **[oo].**

Start on the dot. Trace the dotted line. Use the arrow as a guide.

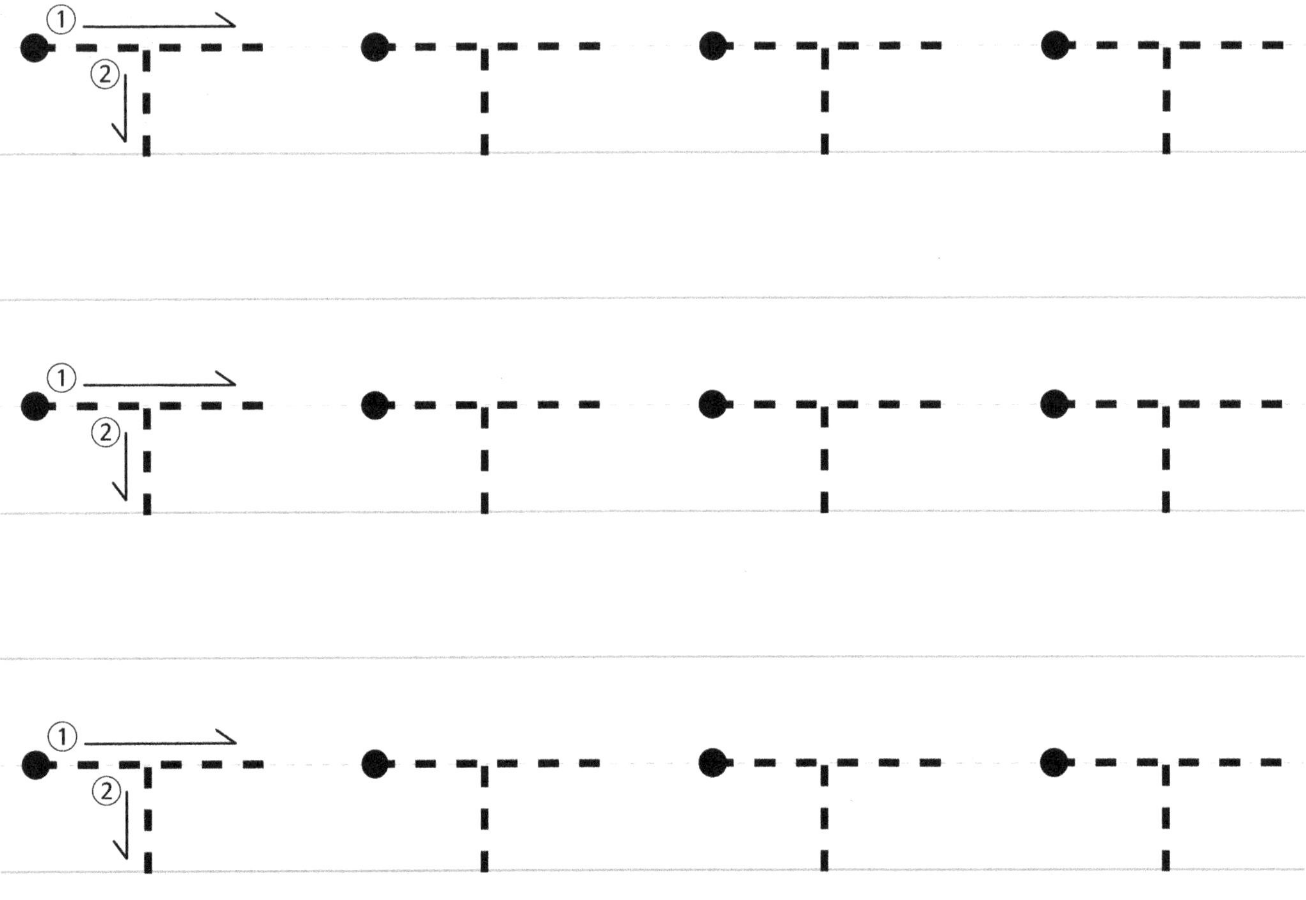

Trace it! Start at the dot! Write it!

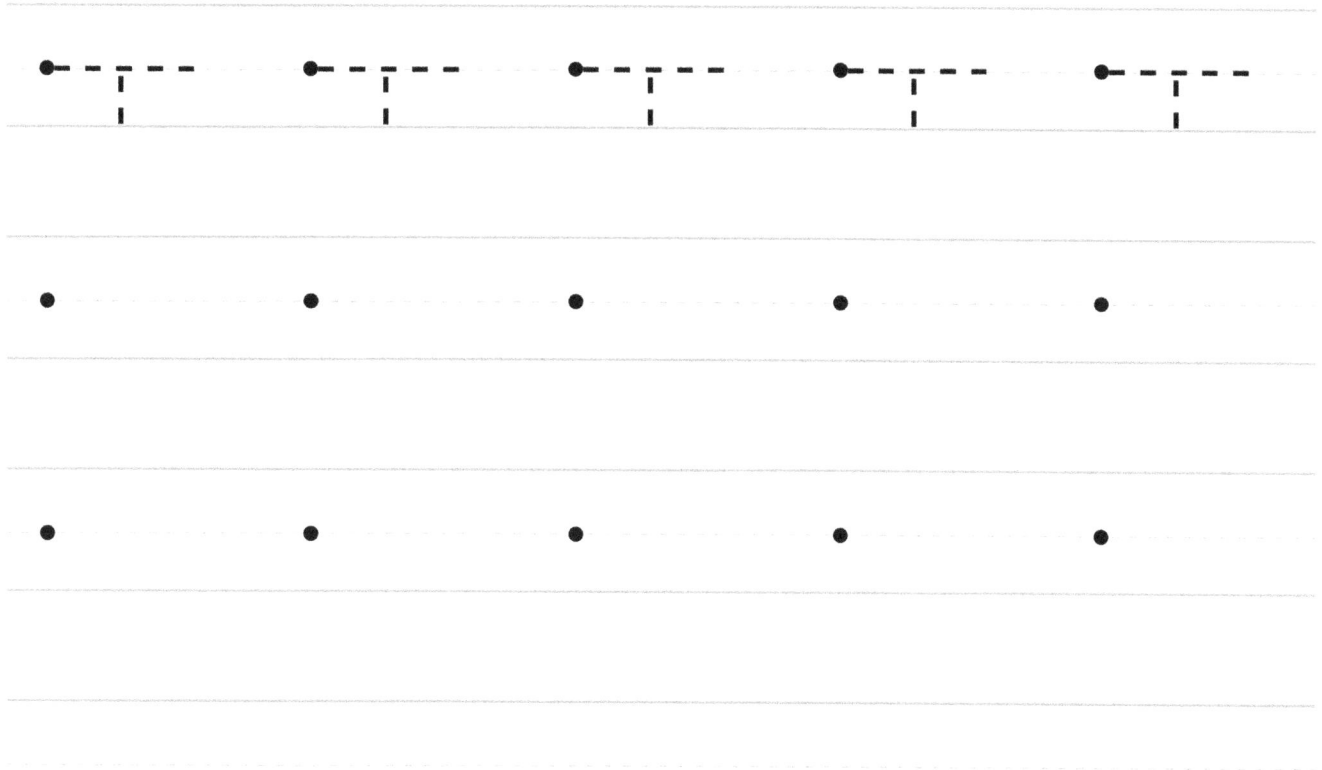

Trace the letter. Trace the word.

[goo-room]

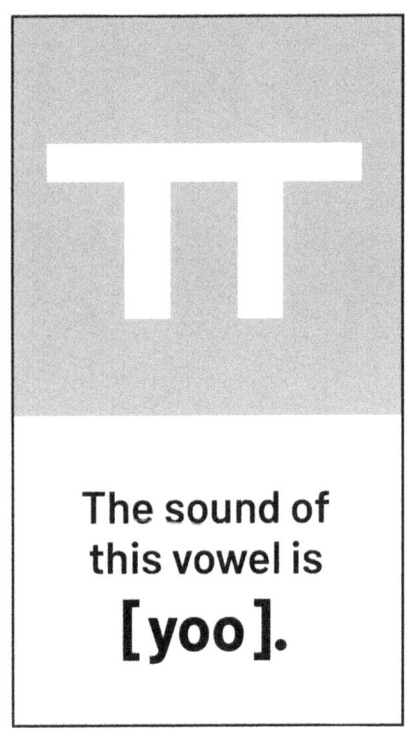

ㅠ is for 우유
[oo-yoo]
milk

The sound of this vowel is **[yoo]**.

Start on the dot. Trace the dotted line. Use the arrow as a guide.

Trace it! Start at the dot! Write it!

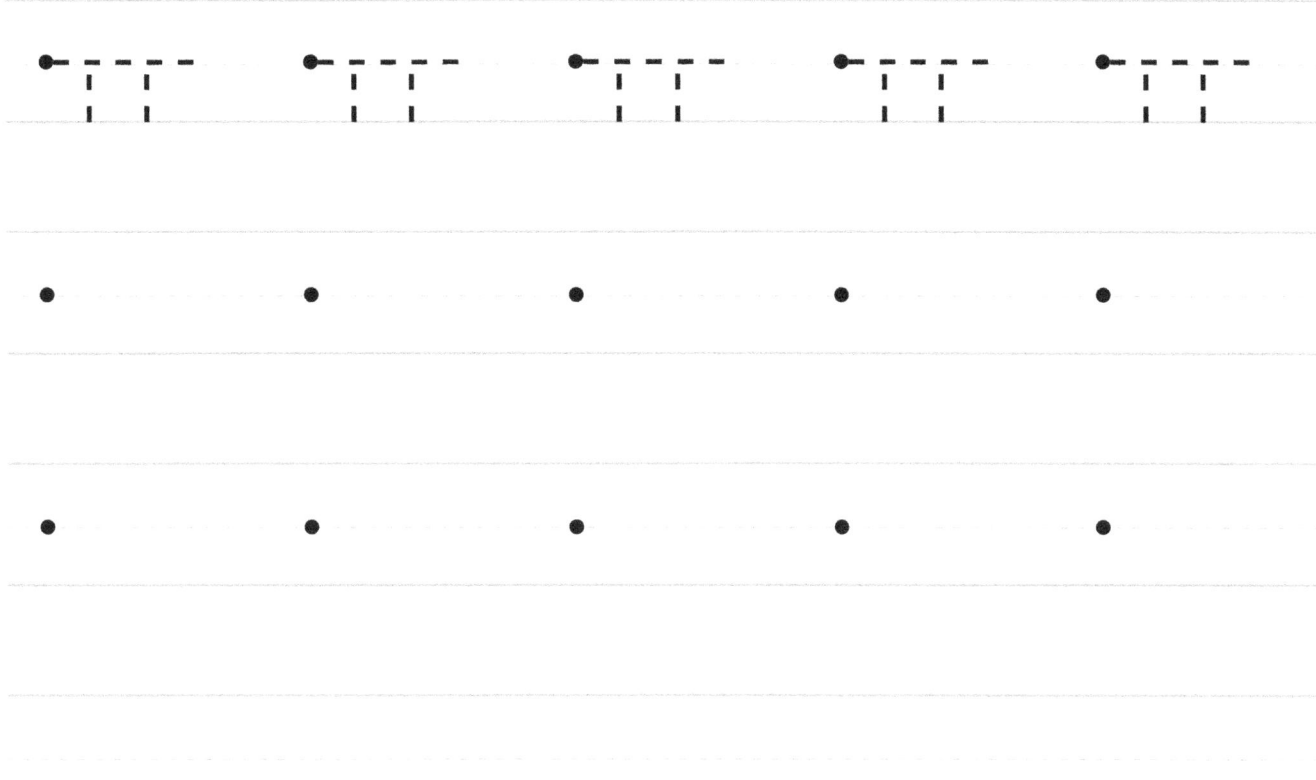

Trace the letter. Trace the word.

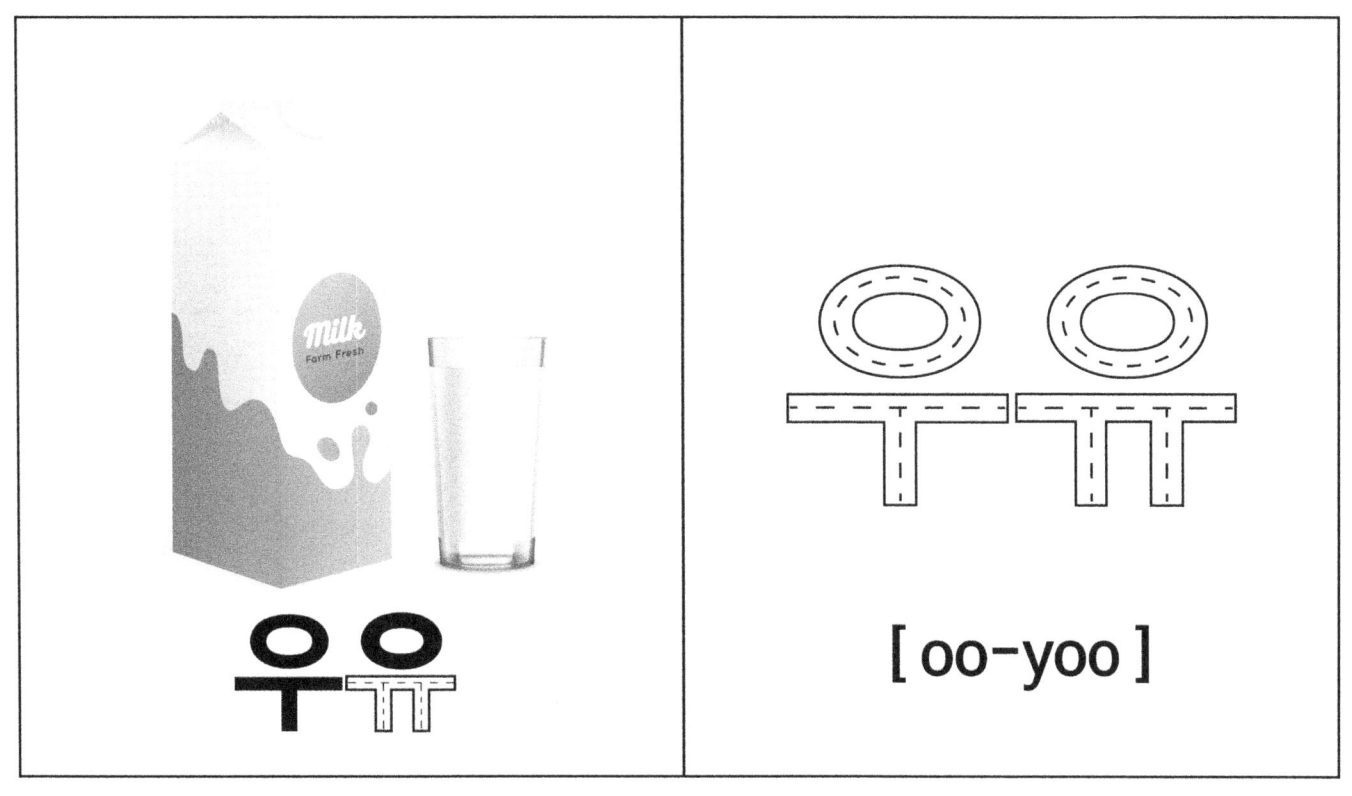

[oo-yoo]

― is for **아이스크림**
[ah-ee-su-ku-reem]
ice cream

The sound of this vowel is **[euh]**.

Start on the dot. Trace the dotted line. Use the arrow as a guide.

Trace it! Start at the dot! Write it!

Trace the letter. Trace the word.

[ah-ee-su-ku-reem]

ㅣ

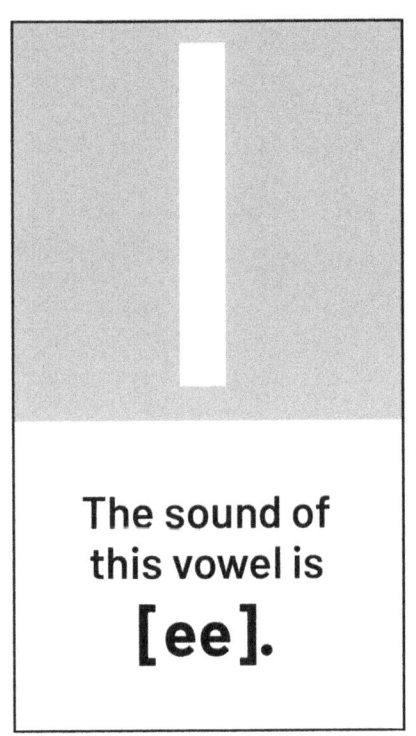

The sound of this vowel is

[ee].

ㅣ is for **시계**

[shee-gae]

clock

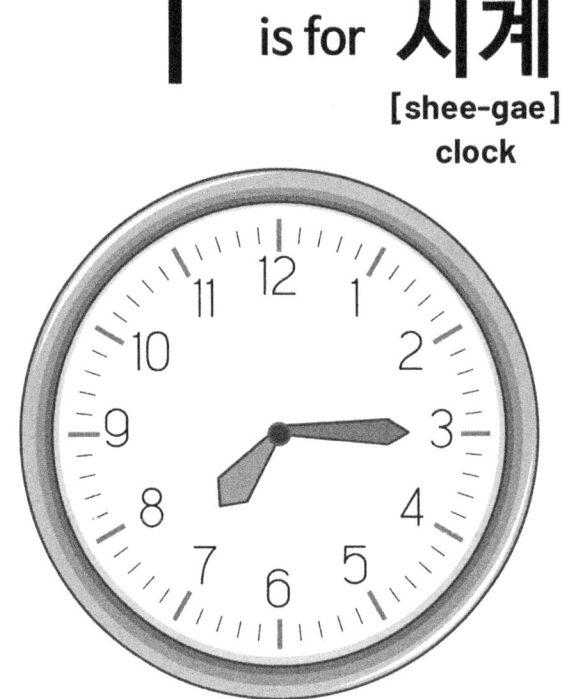

Start on the dot. Trace the dotted line. Use the arrow as a guide.

①

①

①

Trace it! Start at the dot! Write it!

Trace the letter. Trace the word.

[shee-gae]

UNIT 4

쌍모음
Double Vowels

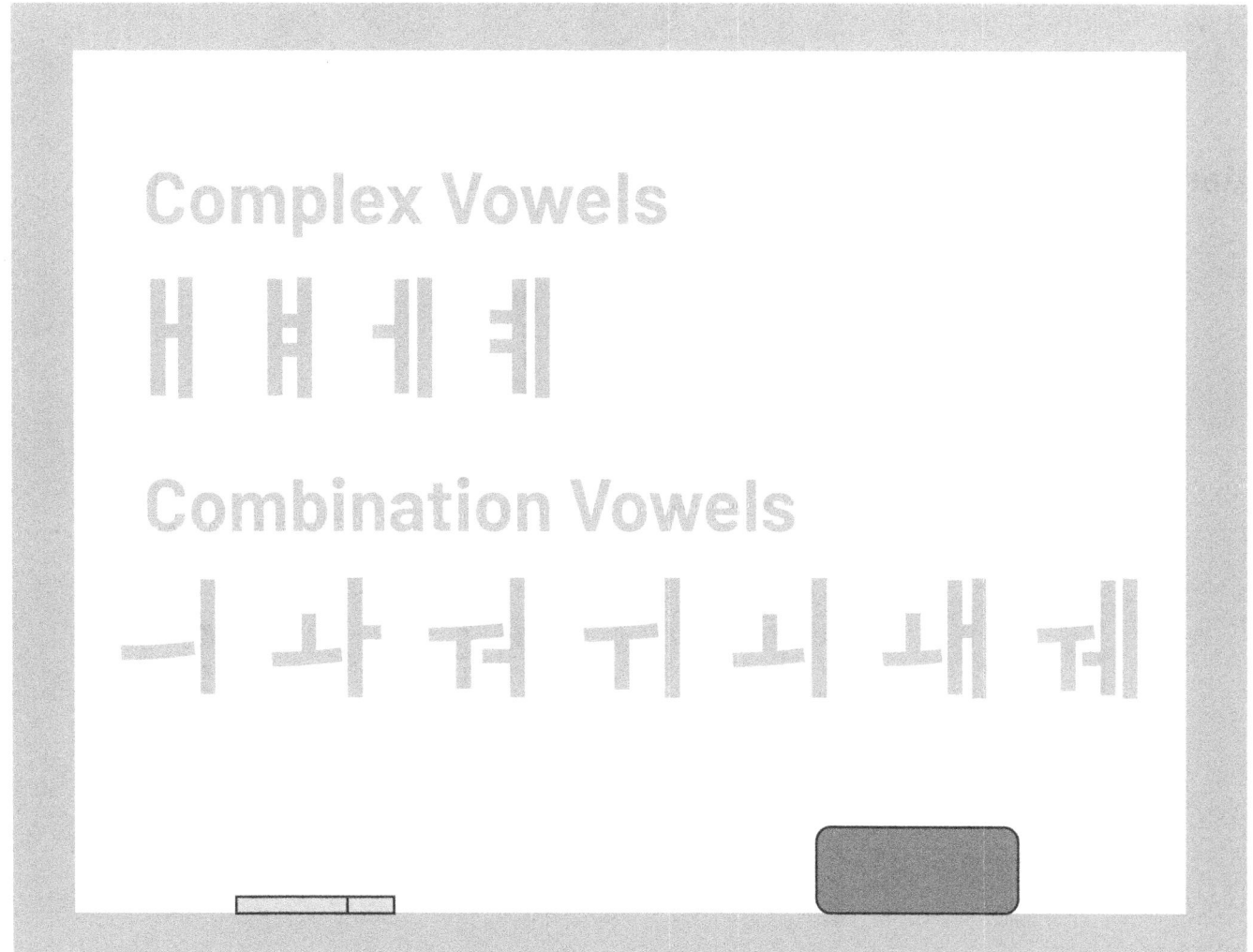

Note: In this unit, we will learn how to write the 11 double vowels.

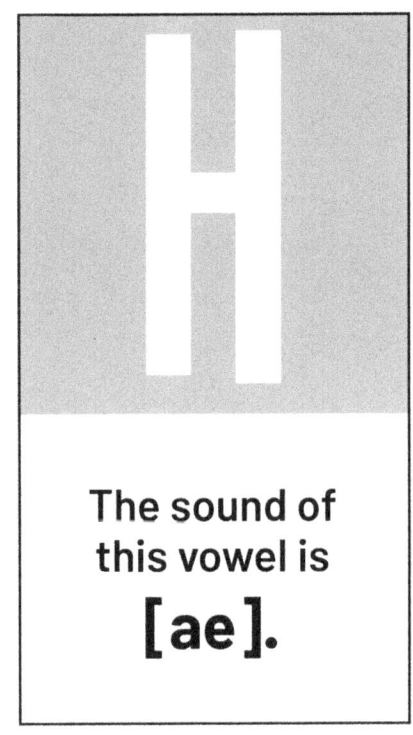

The sound of this vowel is **[ae]**.

H is for 해바라기
[hae-ba-ra-gi]
sunflower

Start on the dot. Trace the dotted line. Use the arrow as a guide.

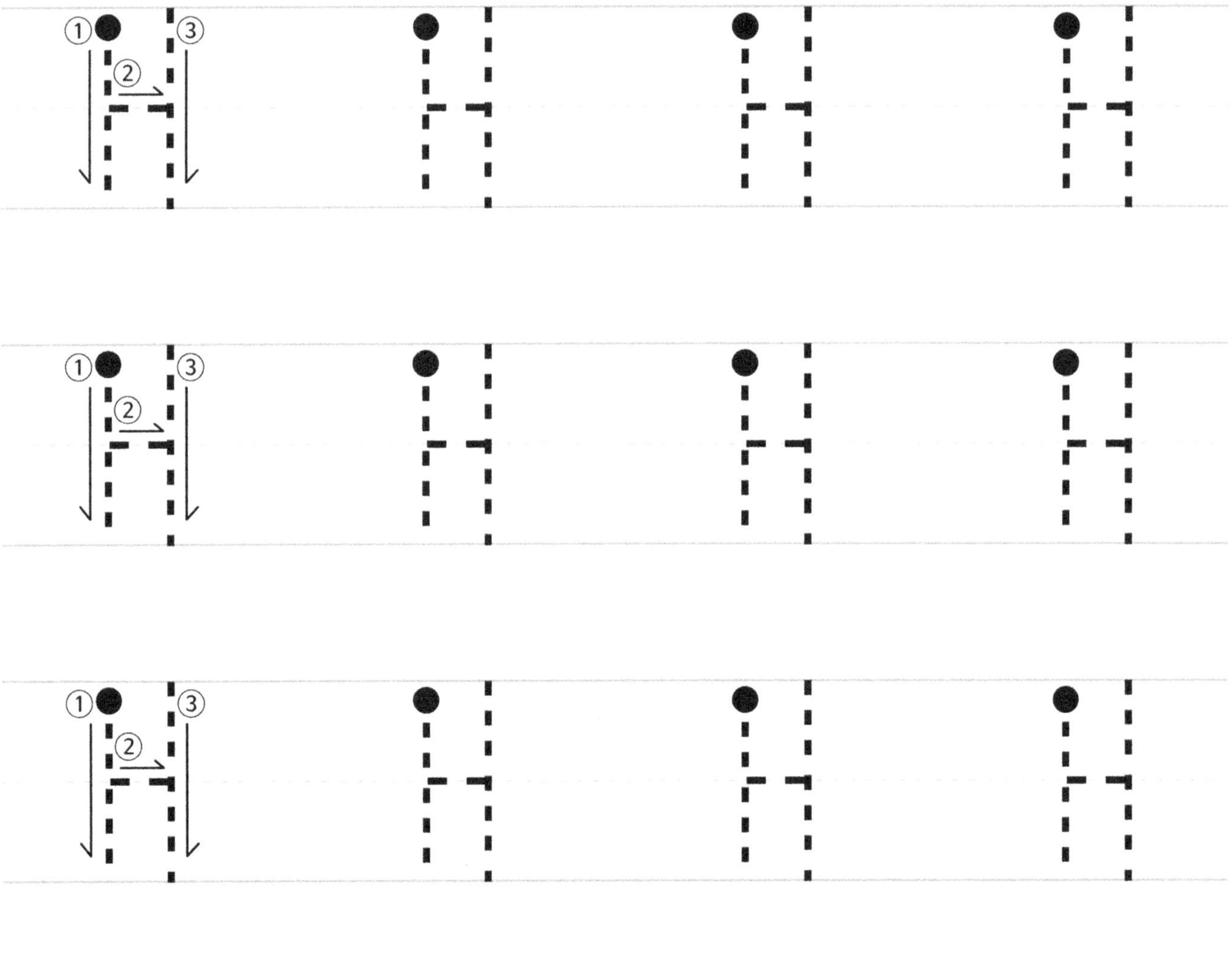

Trace it! Start at the dot! Write it!

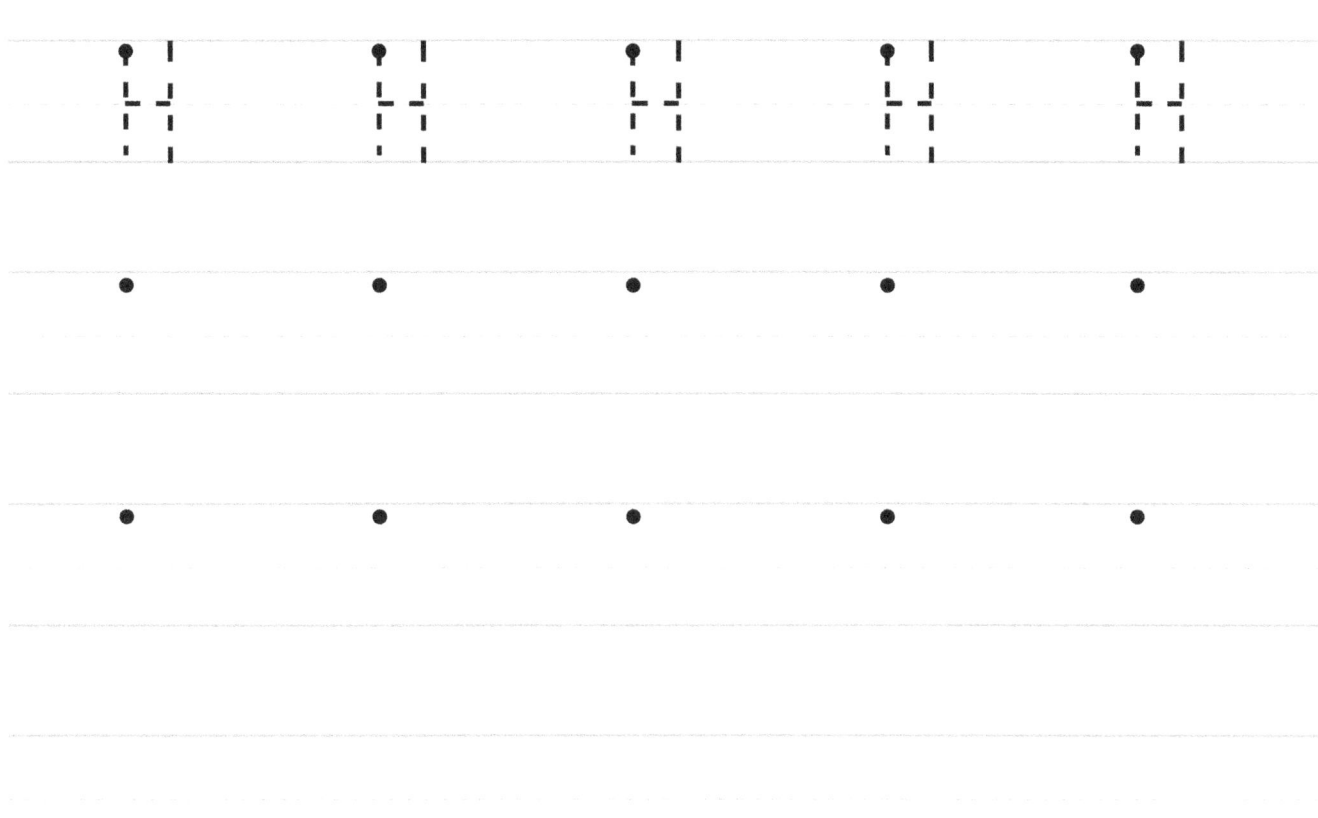

Trace the letter. Trace the word.

[hae-ba-ra-gi]

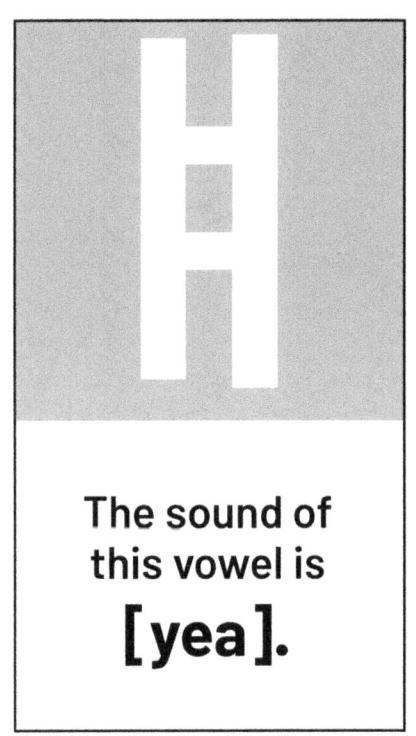

The sound of this vowel is
[yea].

ㅒ is for **얘기책**
[yea-gi-chek]
storybook

Start on the dot. Trace the dotted line. Use the arrow as a guide.

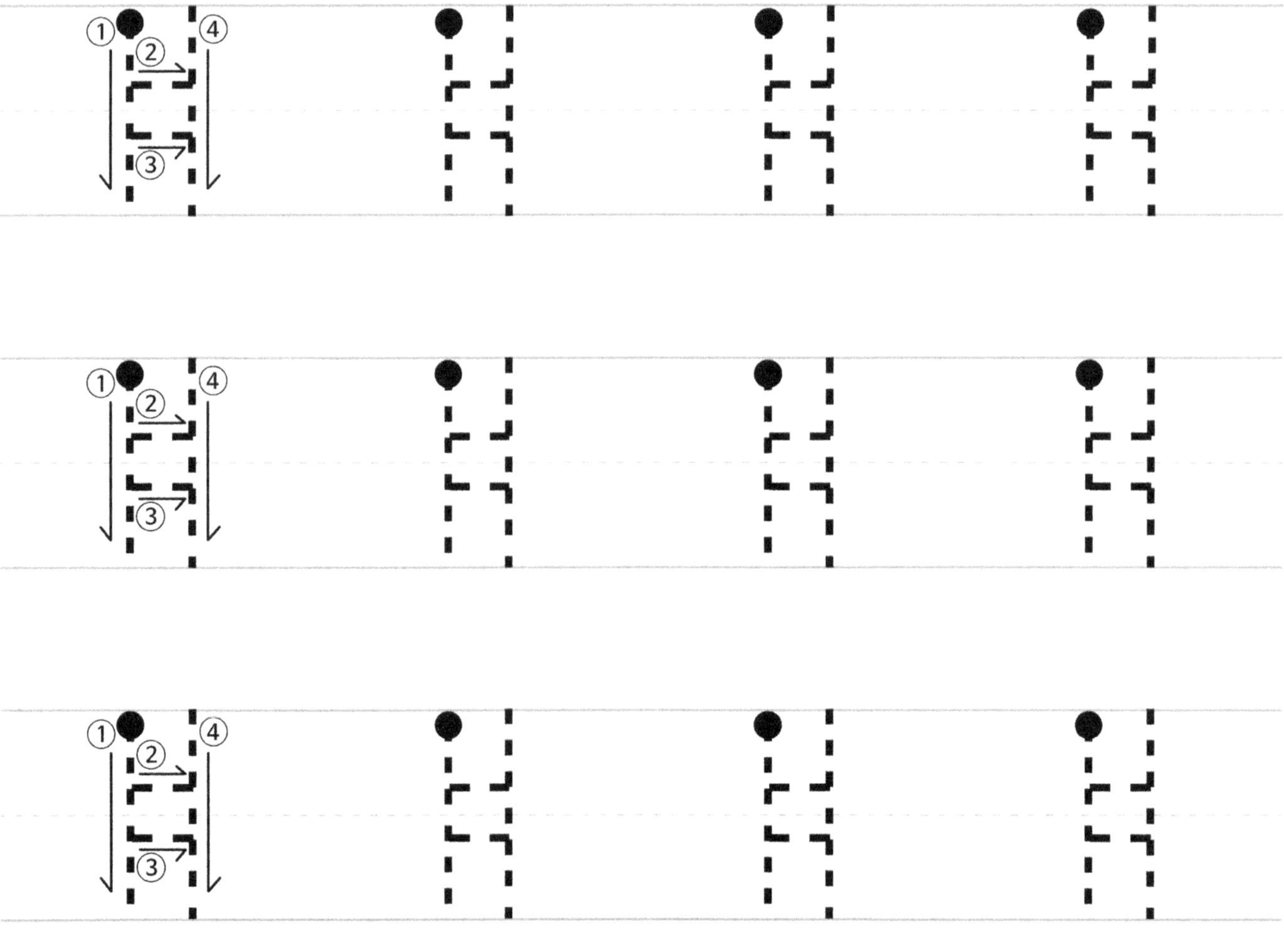

Trace it! Start at the dot! Write it!

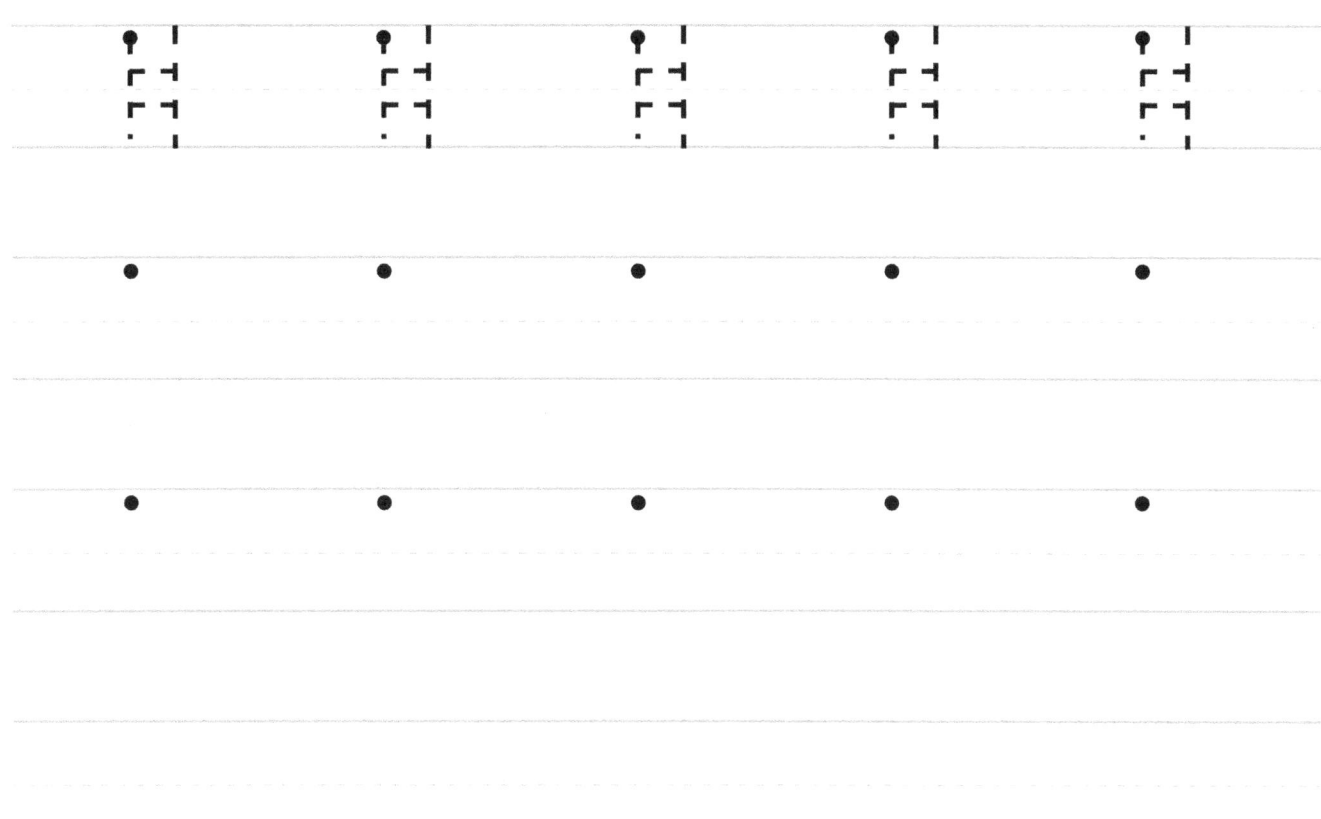

Trace the letter. Trace the word.

애기책

[yea-gi]

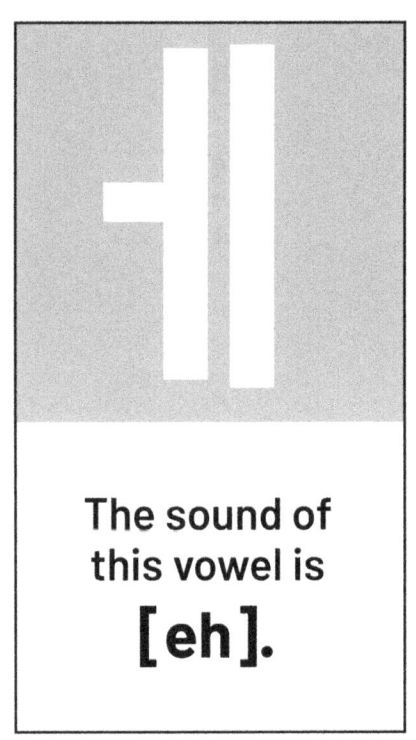

ㅔ is for 케이크
[keh-ee-kuh]
cake

The sound of this vowel is **[eh]**.

Start on the dot. Trace the dotted line. Use the arrow as a guide.

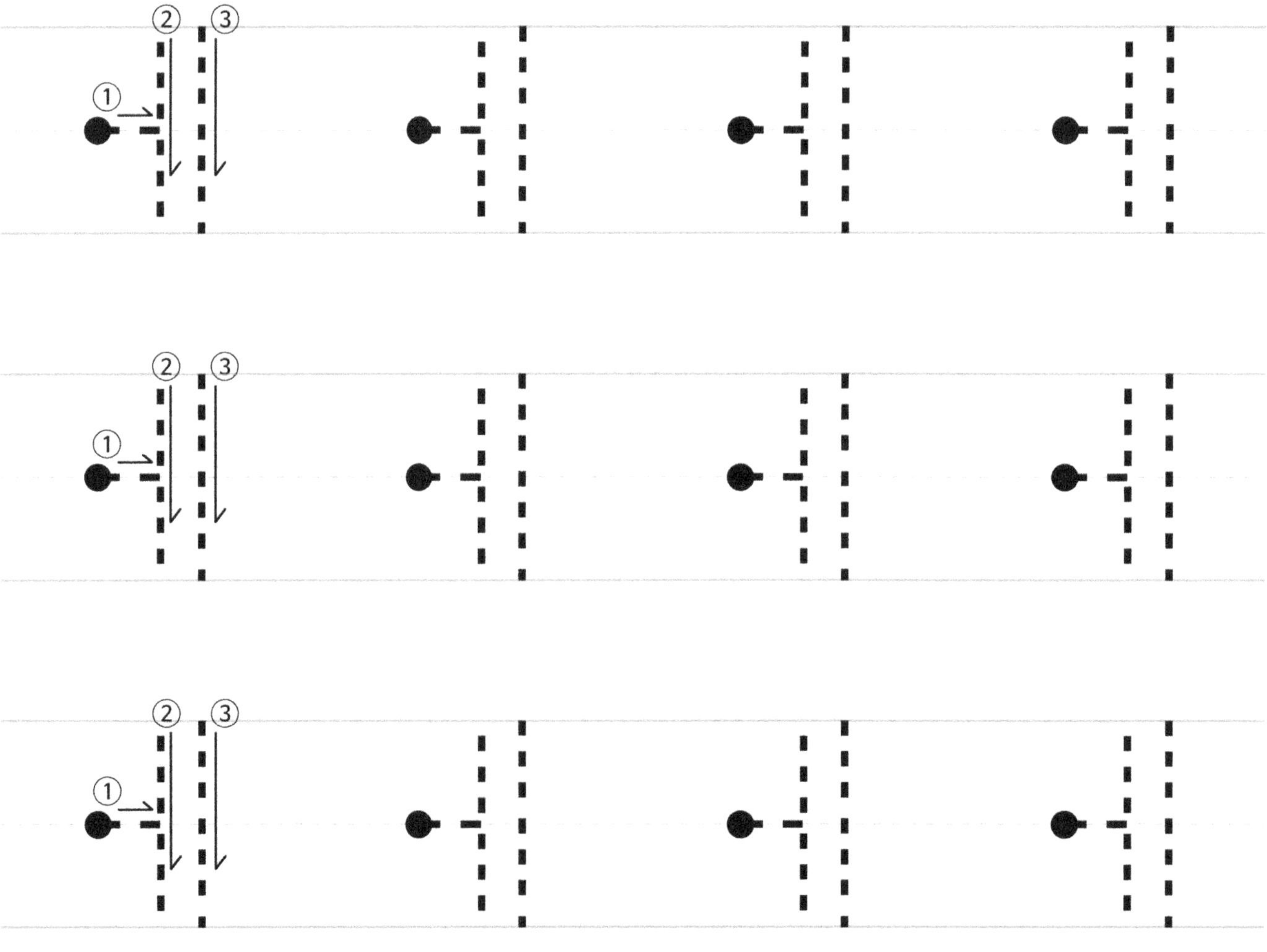

Trace it! Start at the dot! Write it!

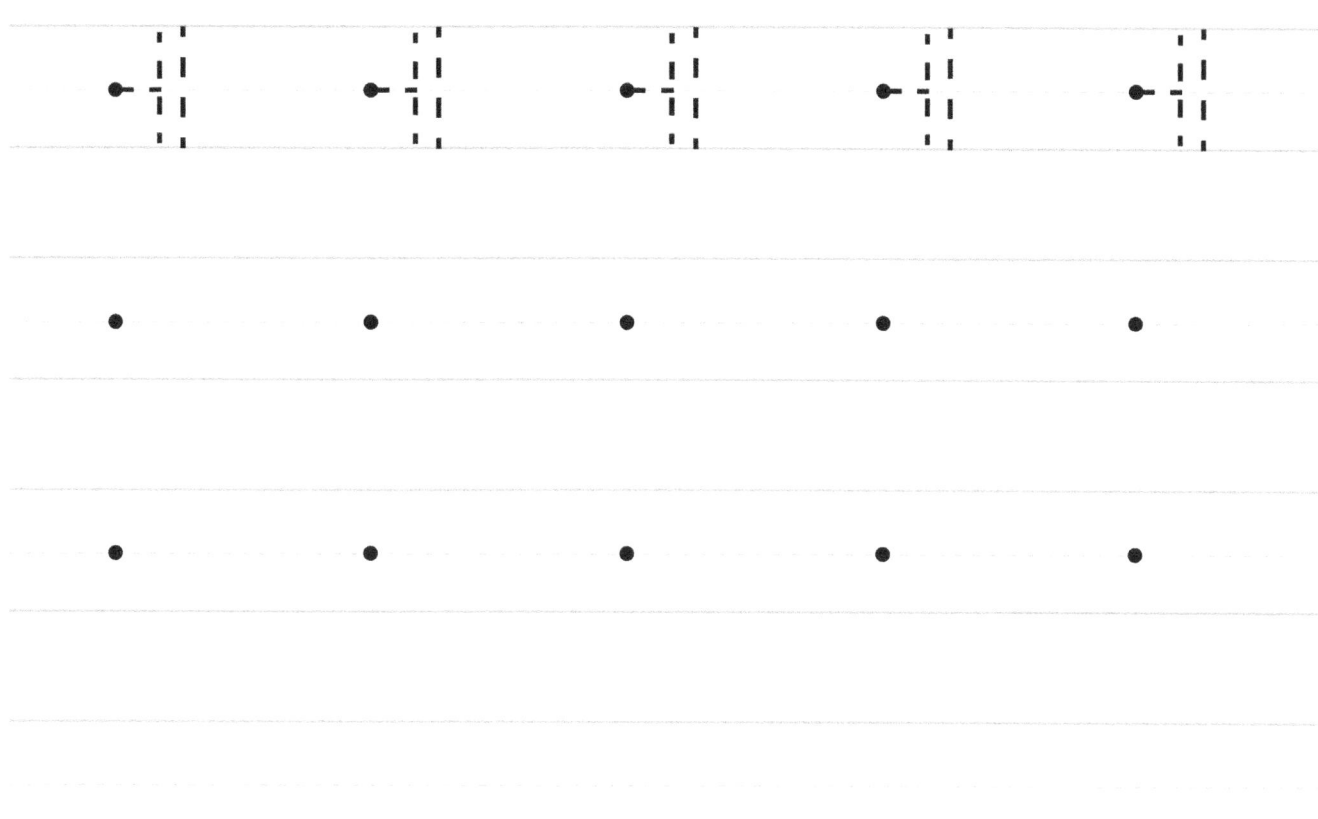

Trace the letter. Trace the word.

케이크

[keh-ee-kuh]

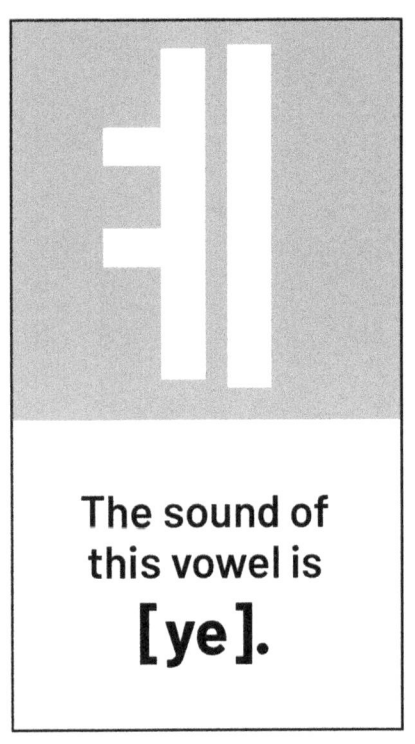

The sound of this vowel is **[ye]**.

ㅖ is for 예수님
[ye-soo-nim]
Jesus

Start on the dot. Trace the dotted line. Use the arrow as a guide.

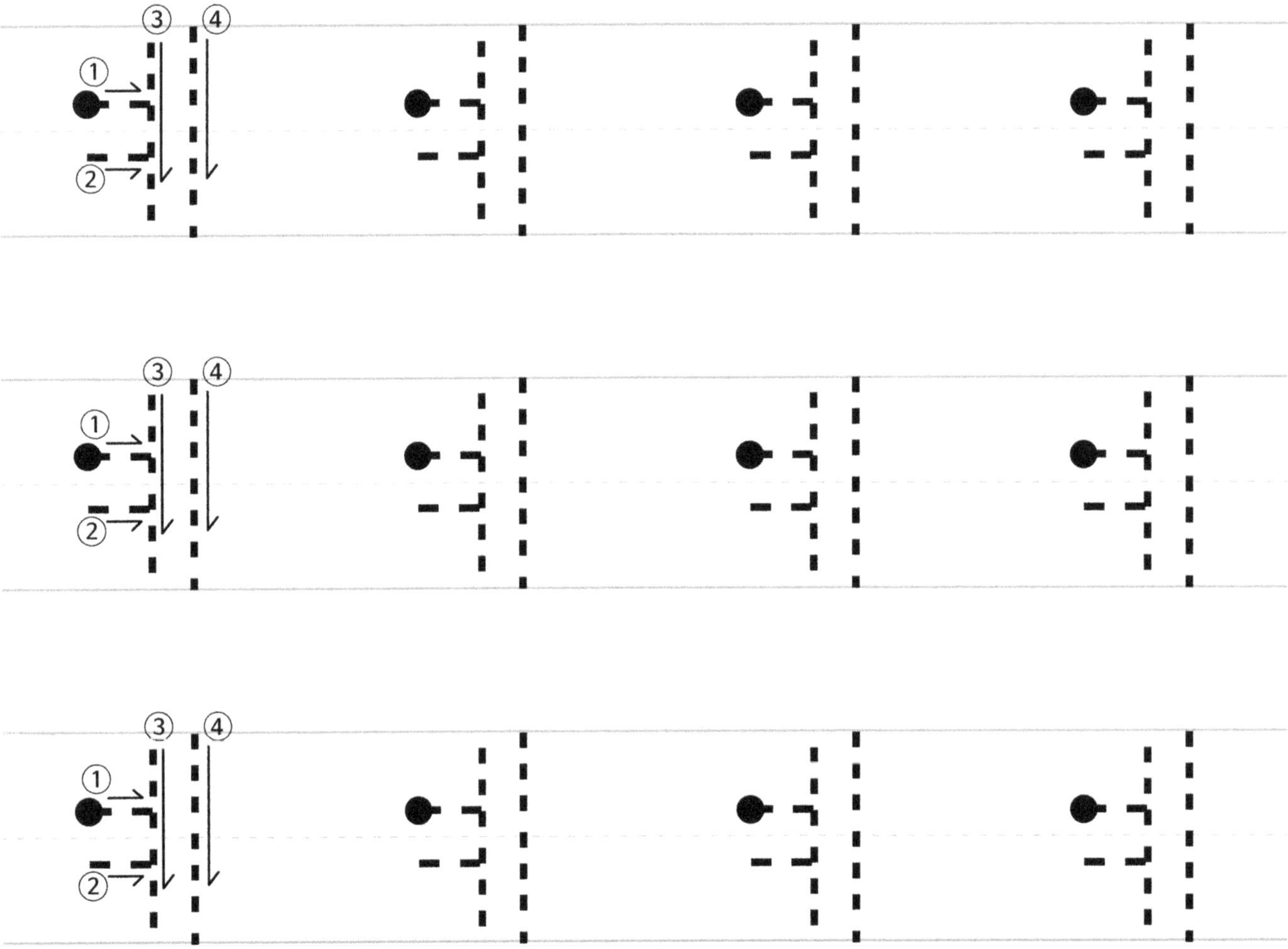

Trace it! Start at the dot! Write it!

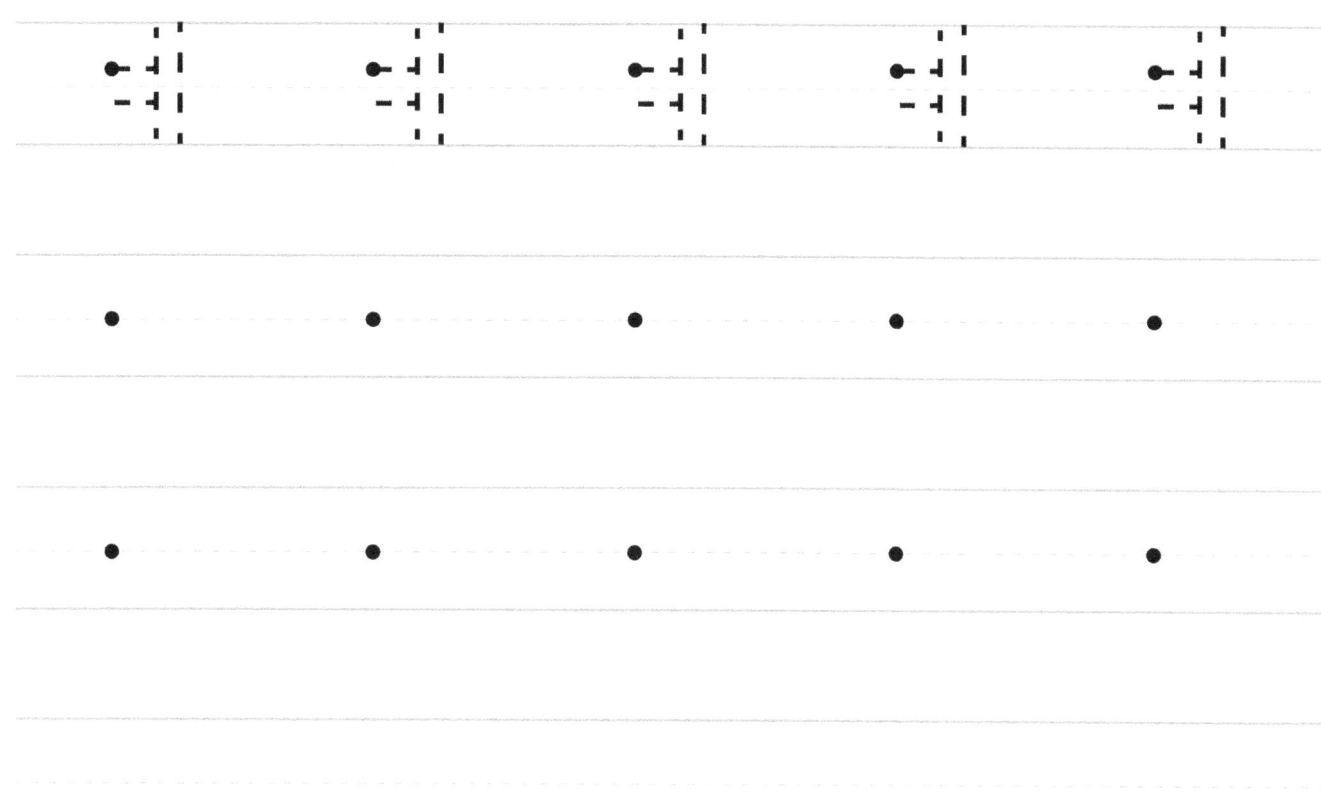

Trace the letter. Trace the word.

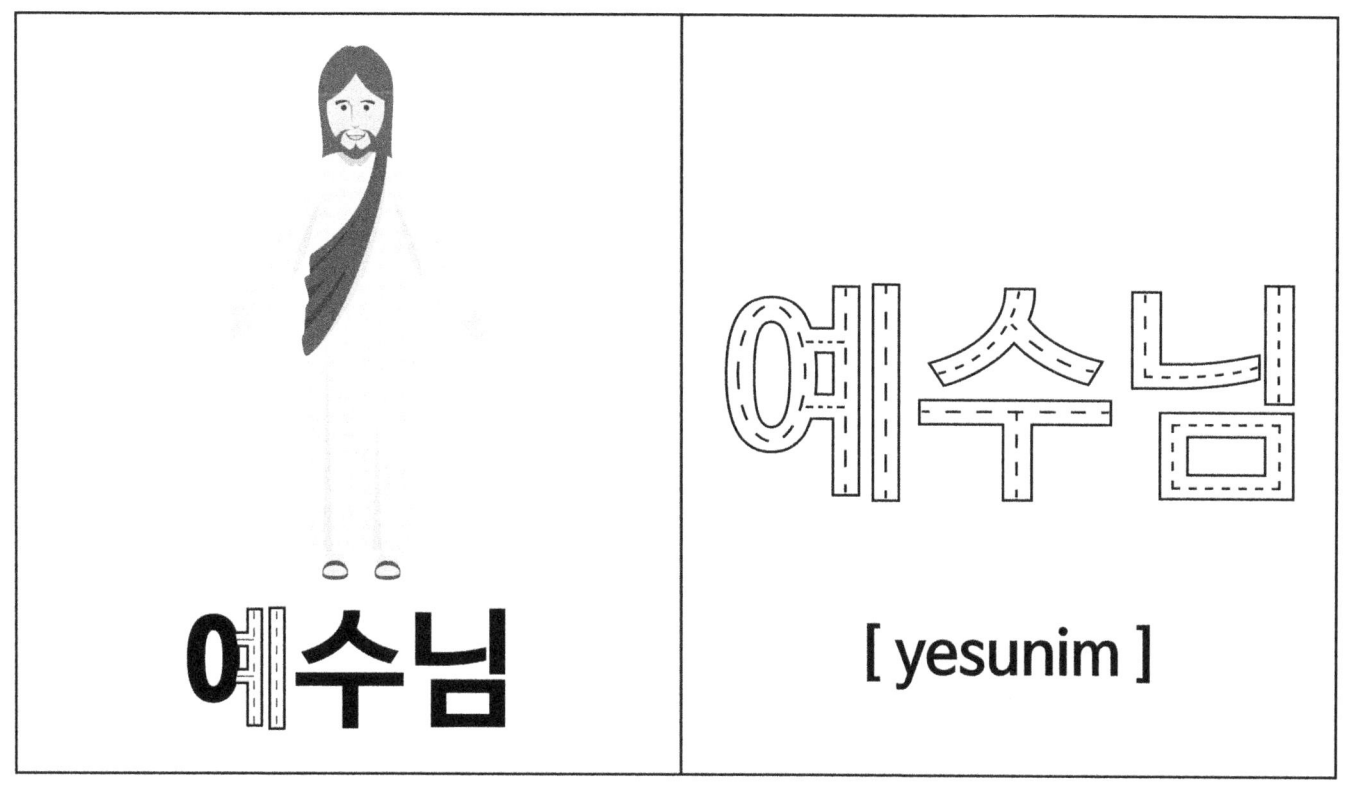

[yesunim]

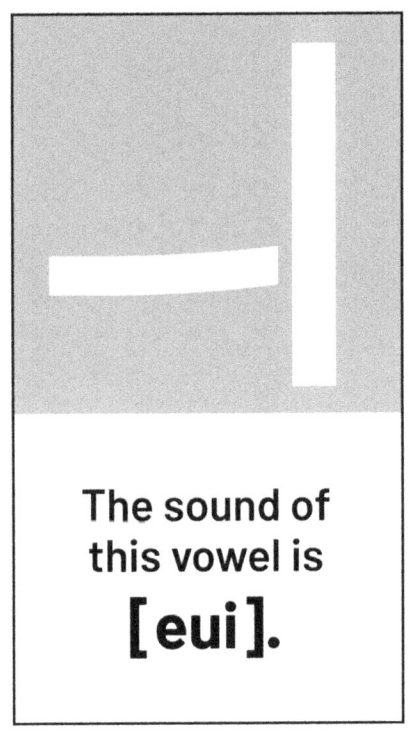

ㅢ is for 의사
[eui-sa]
doctor

The sound of this vowel is **[eui]**.

Start on the dot. Trace the dotted line. Use the arrow as a guide.

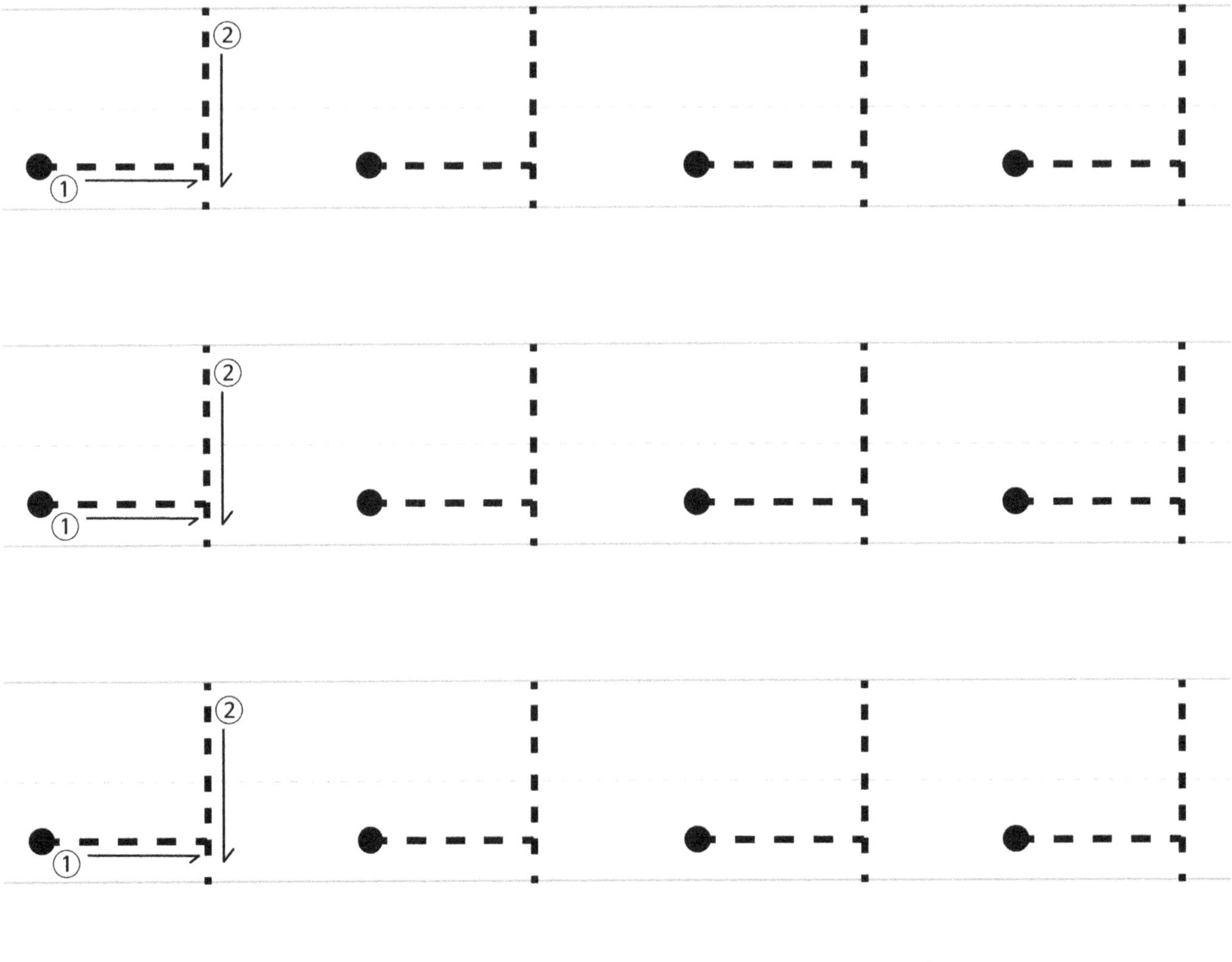

Trace it! Start at the dot! Write it!

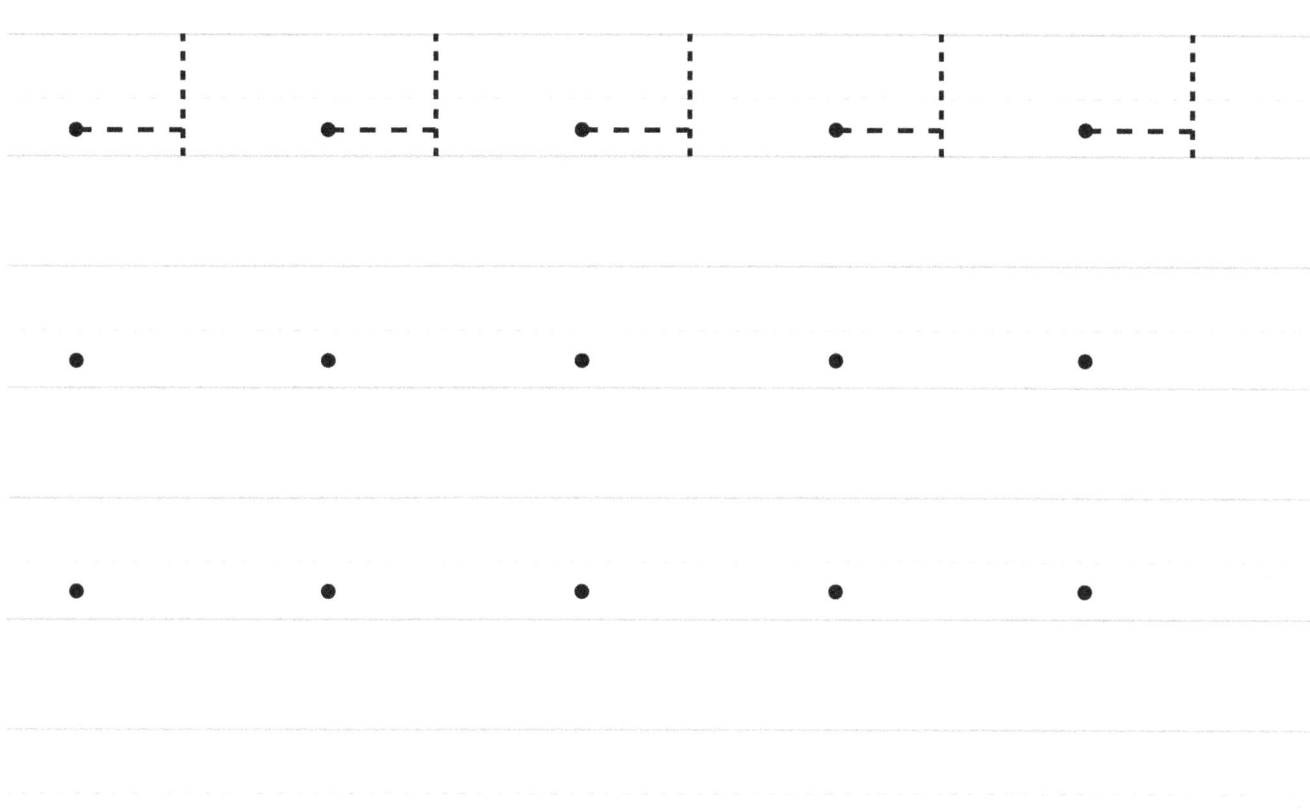

Trace the letter. Trace the word.

의사

[eui-sa]

과

The sound of this vowel is

[wah].

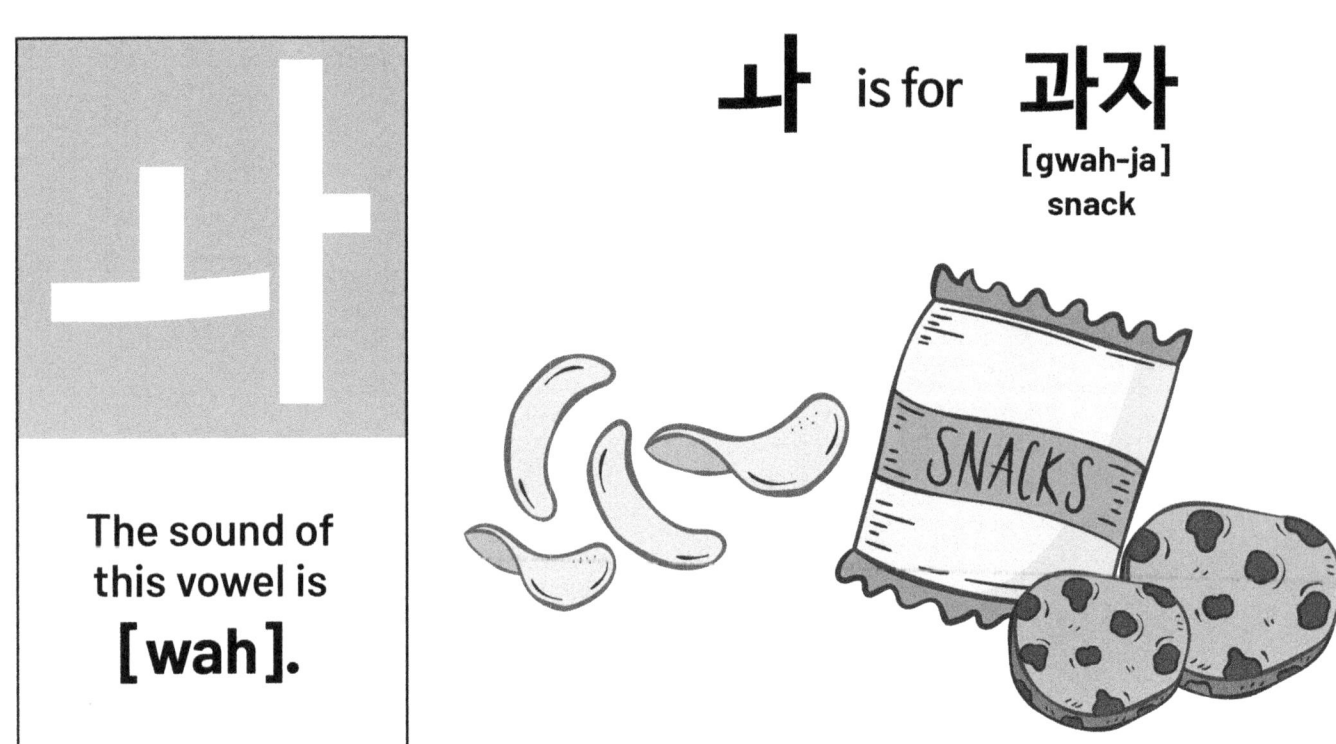

ㅘ is for **과자**
[gwah-ja]
snack

Start on the dot. Trace the dotted line. Use the arrow as a guide.

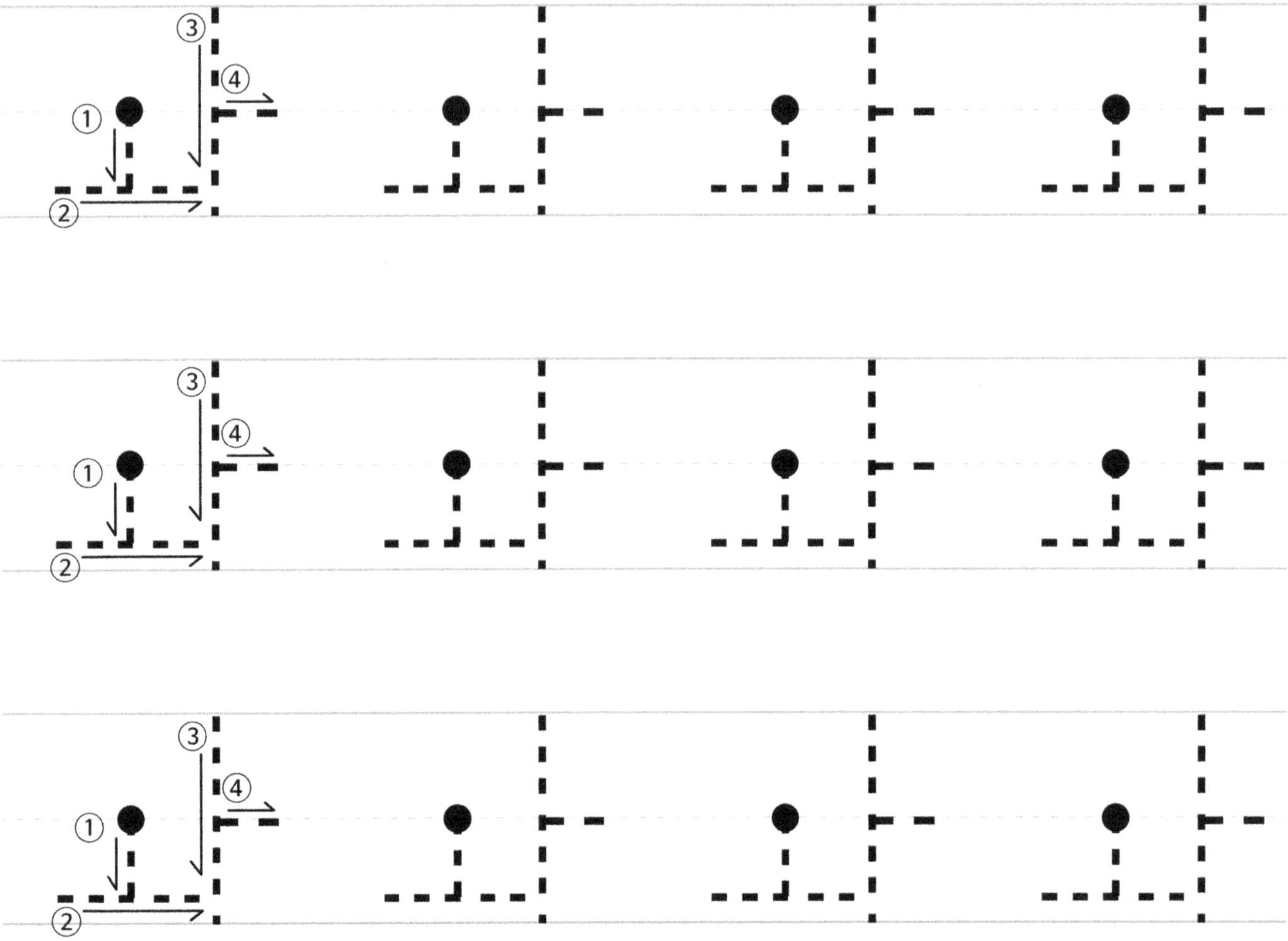

Trace it! Start at the dot! Write it!

Trace the letter. Trace the word.

과자

[gwah-ja]

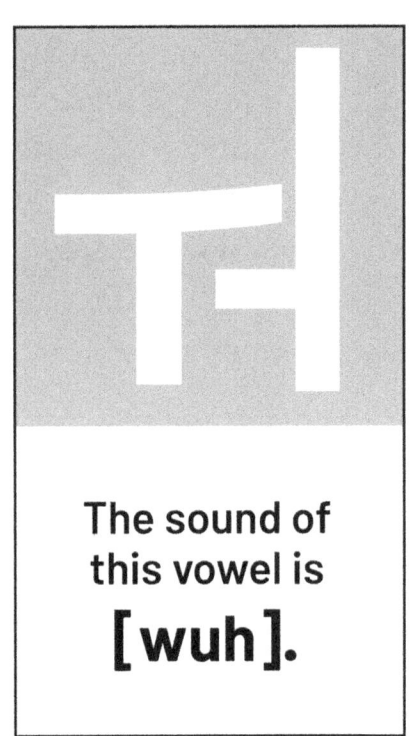

The sound of this vowel is **[wuh]**.

ㅝ is for 샤워
[sha-wuh]
shower

Start on the dot. Trace the dotted line. Use the arrow as a guide.

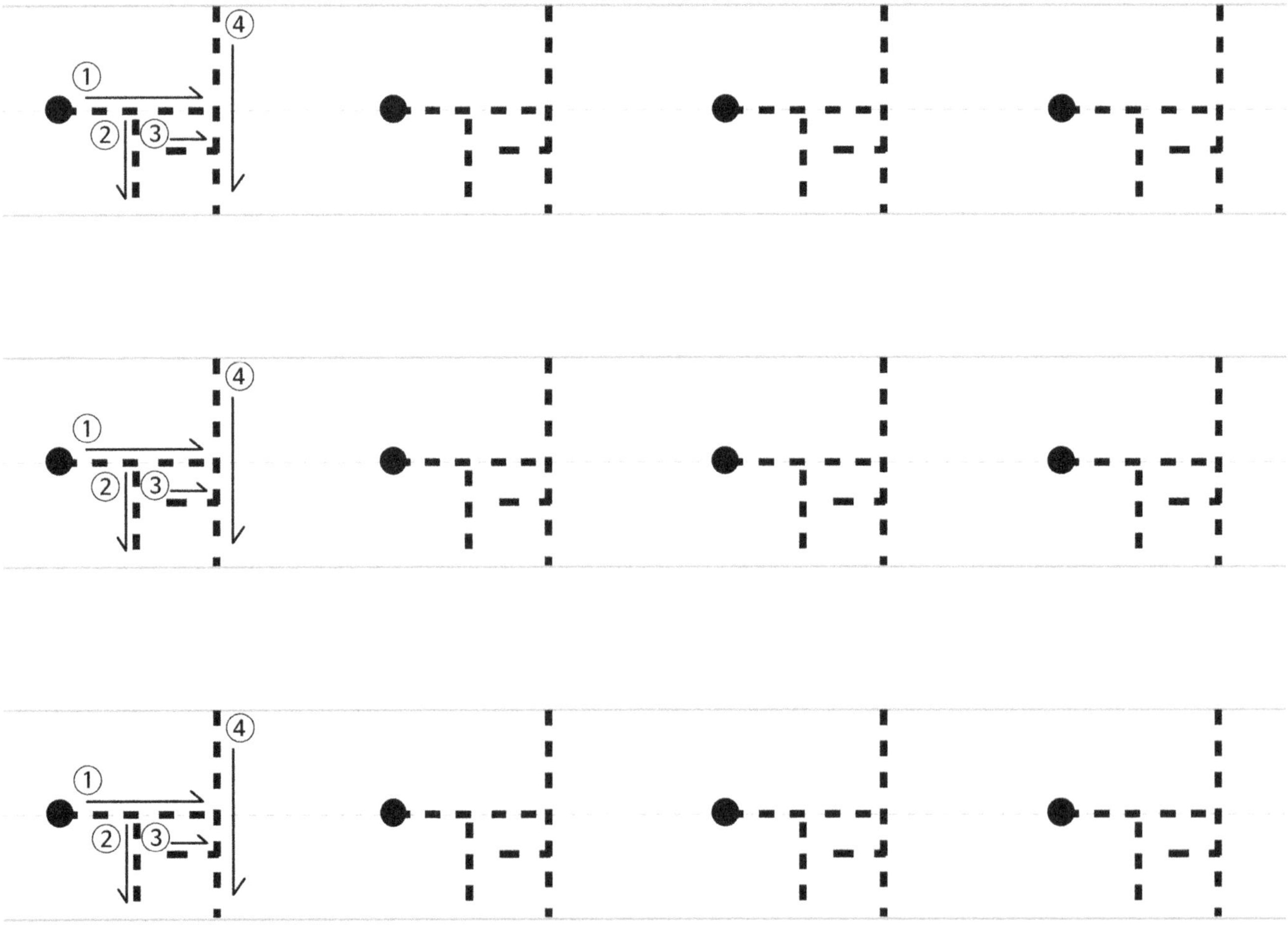

Trace it! Start at the dot! Write it!

Trace the letter. Trace the word.

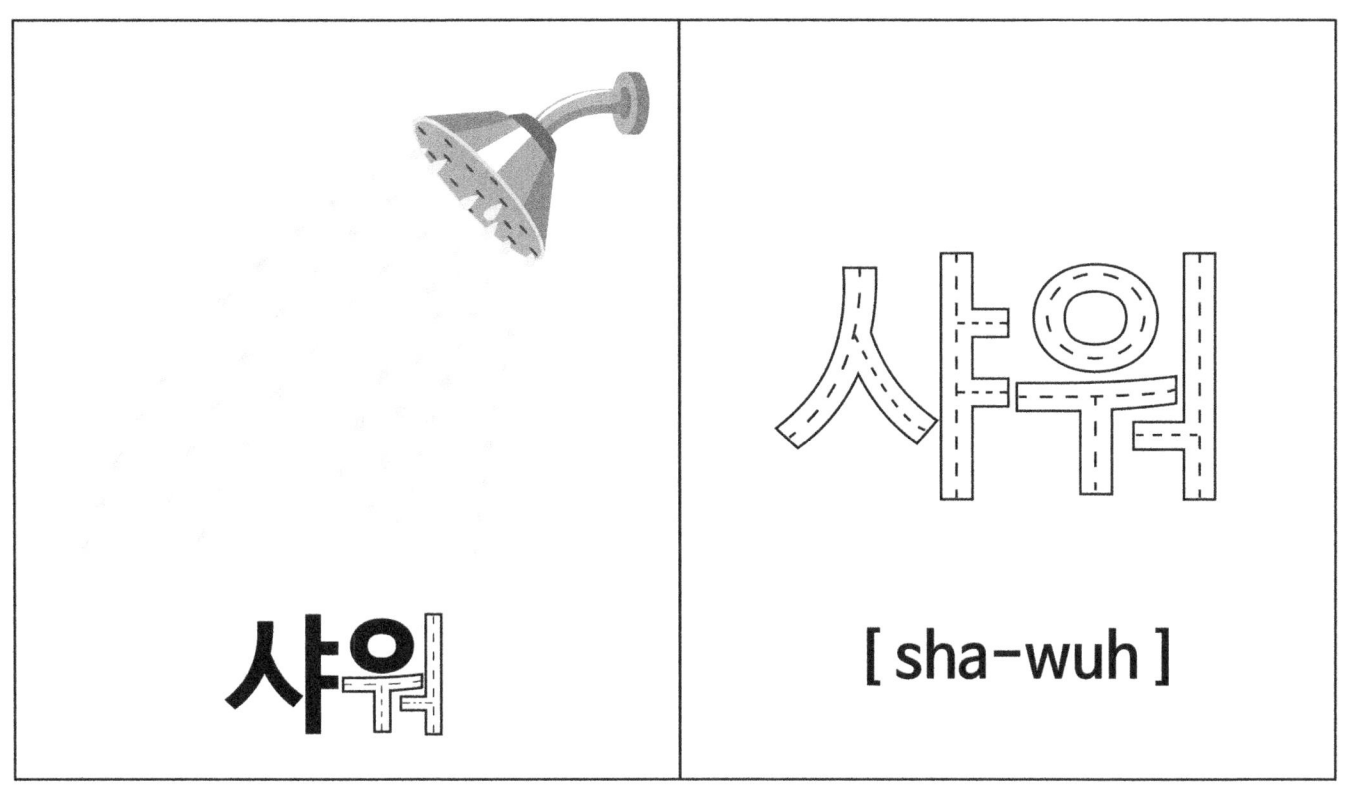

샤워

[sha-wuh]

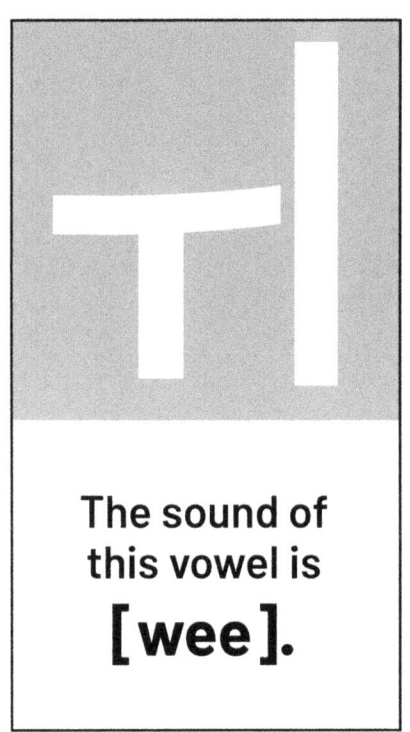

ㅟ is for 주사위
[ju-sa-wee]
dice

The sound of this vowel is **[wee]**.

Start on the dot. Trace the dotted line. Use the arrow as a guide.

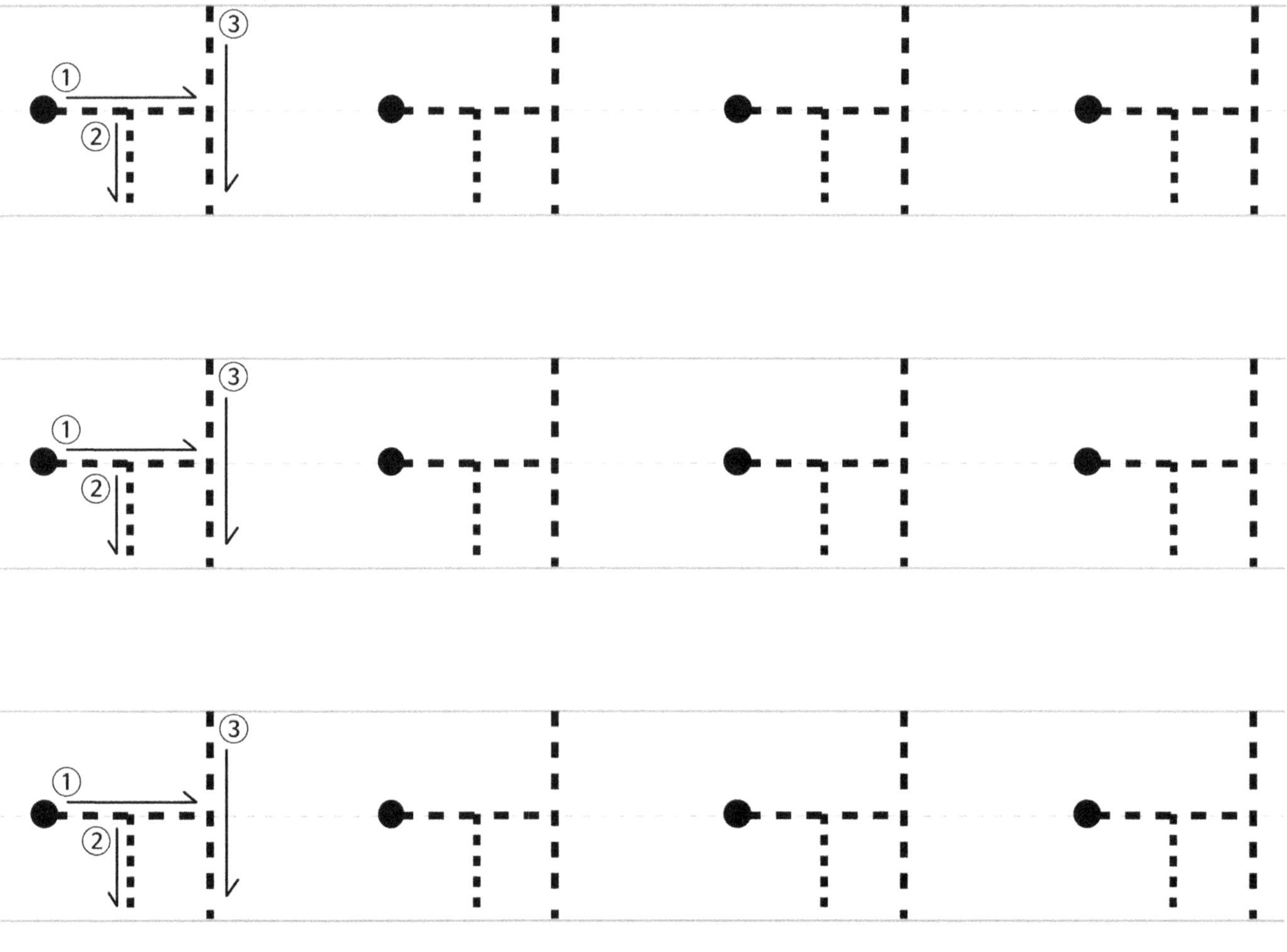

Trace it! Start at the dot! Write it!

Trace the letter. Trace the word.

주사위

[ju-sa-wee]

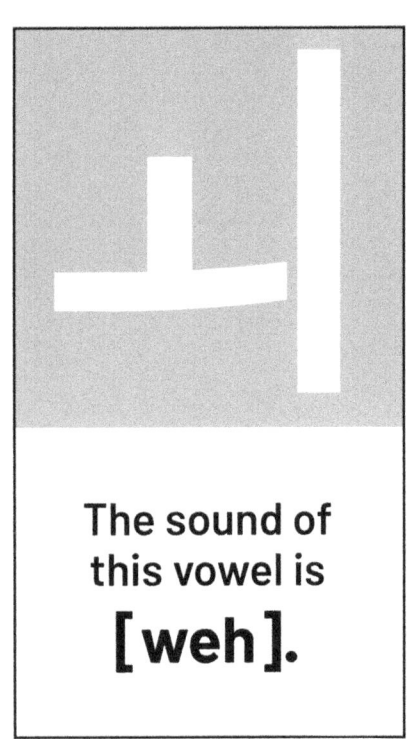

The sound of this vowel is **[weh]**.

ㅚ is for **열쇠**
[yeol-sueh]
key

Start on the dot. Trace the dotted line. Use the arrow as a guide.

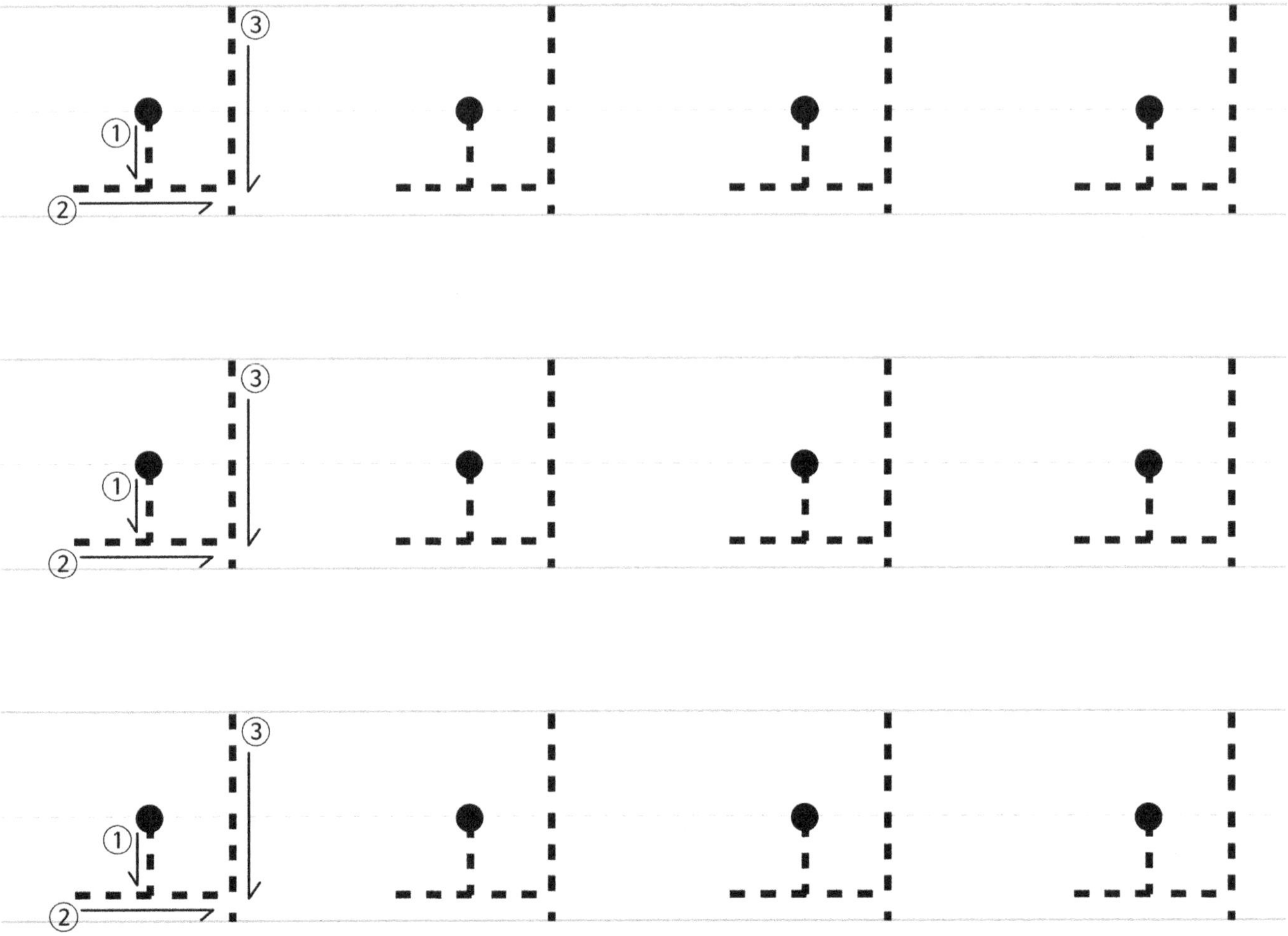

Trace it! Start at the dot! Write it!

Trace the letter. Trace the word.

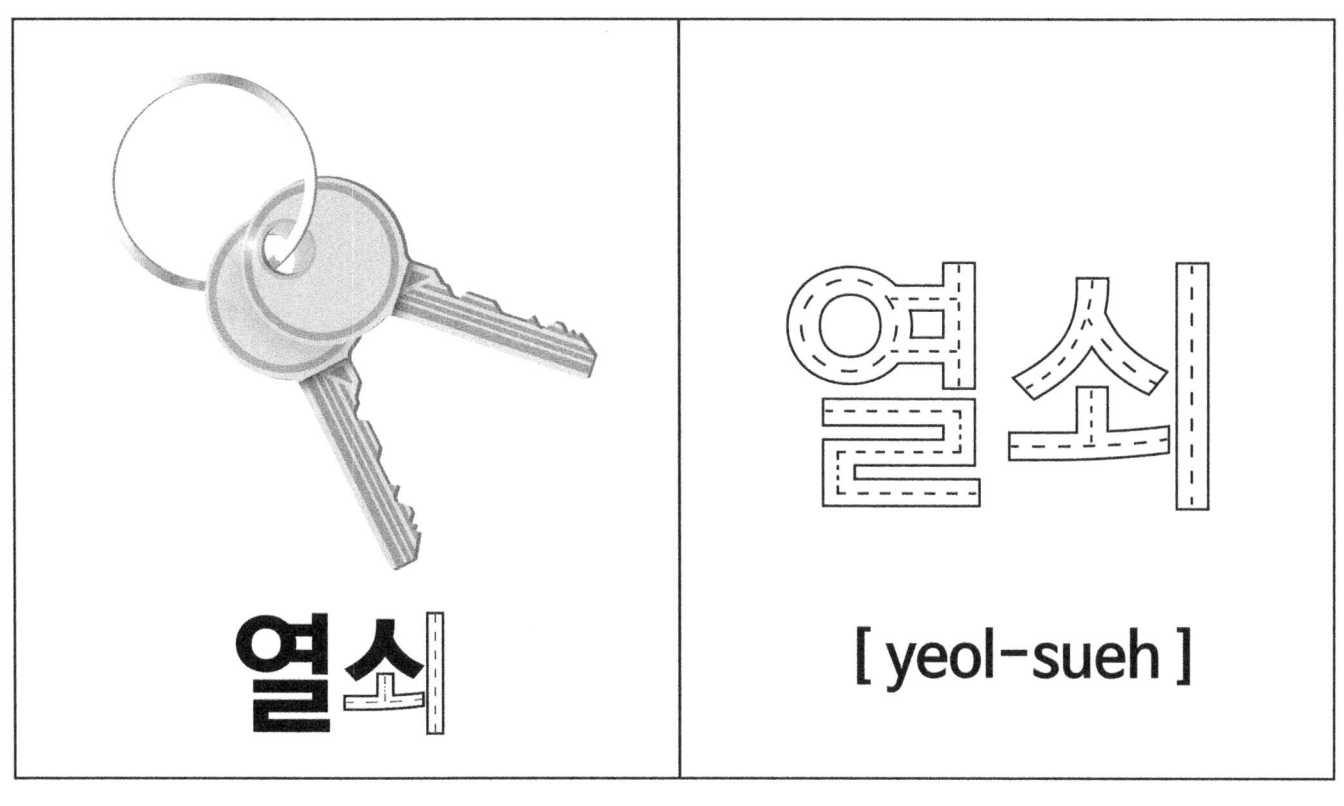

[yeol-sueh]

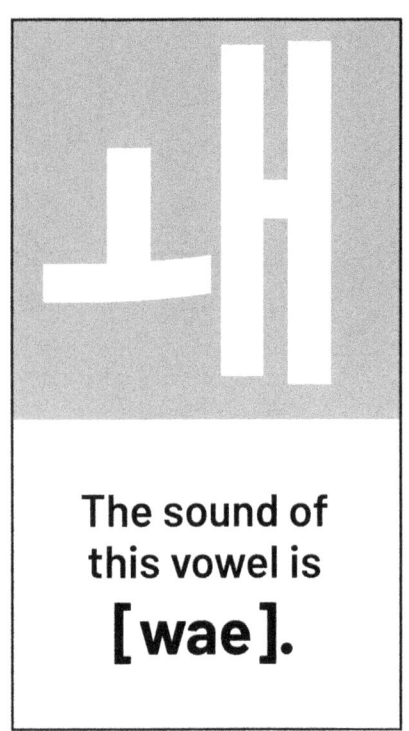

The sound of this vowel is **[wae]**.

ㅙ is for 돼지
[dwae-jee]
pig

Start on the dot. Trace the dotted line. Use the arrow as a guide.

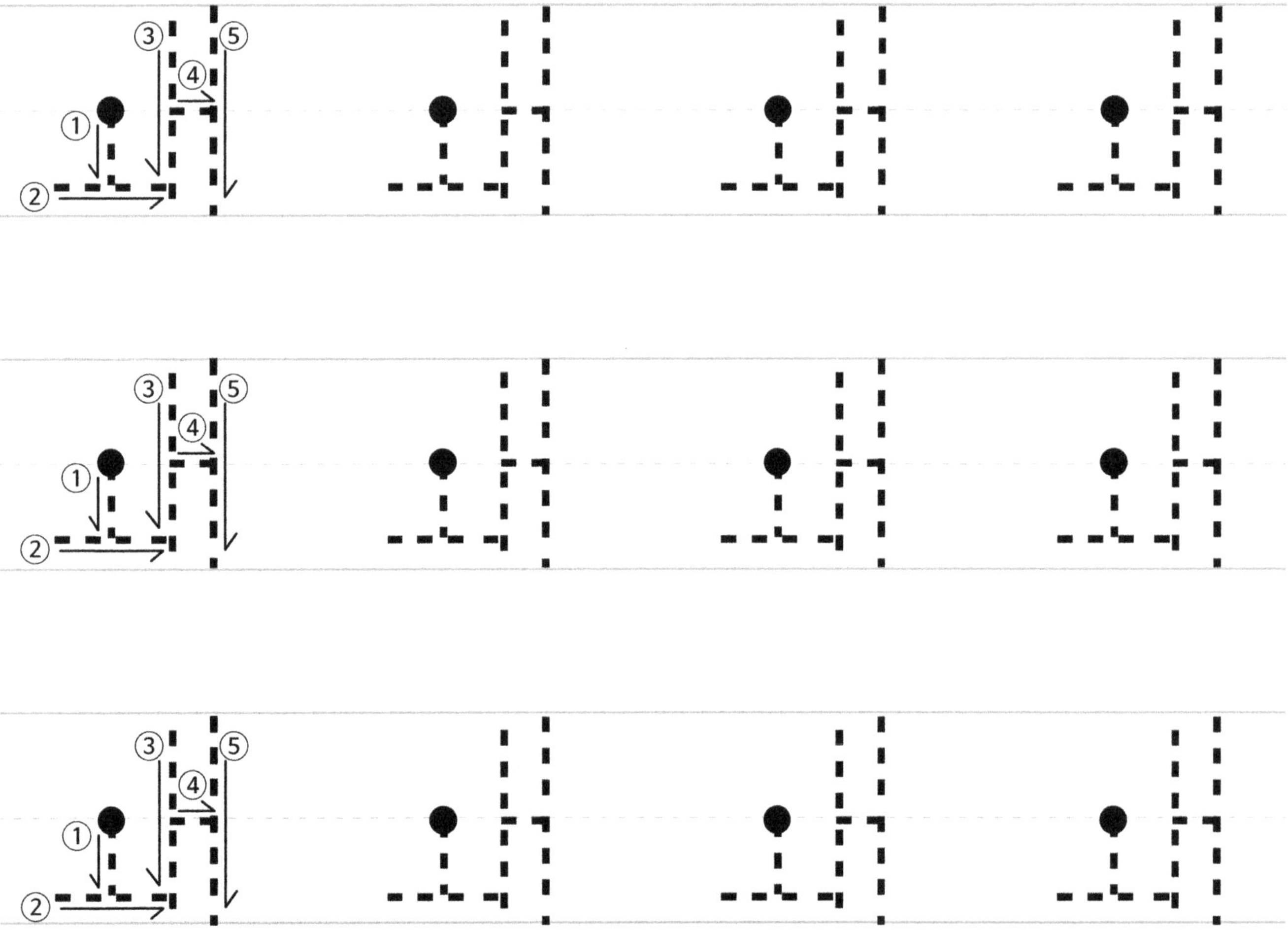

Trace it! Start at the dot! Write it!

Trace the letter. Trace the word.

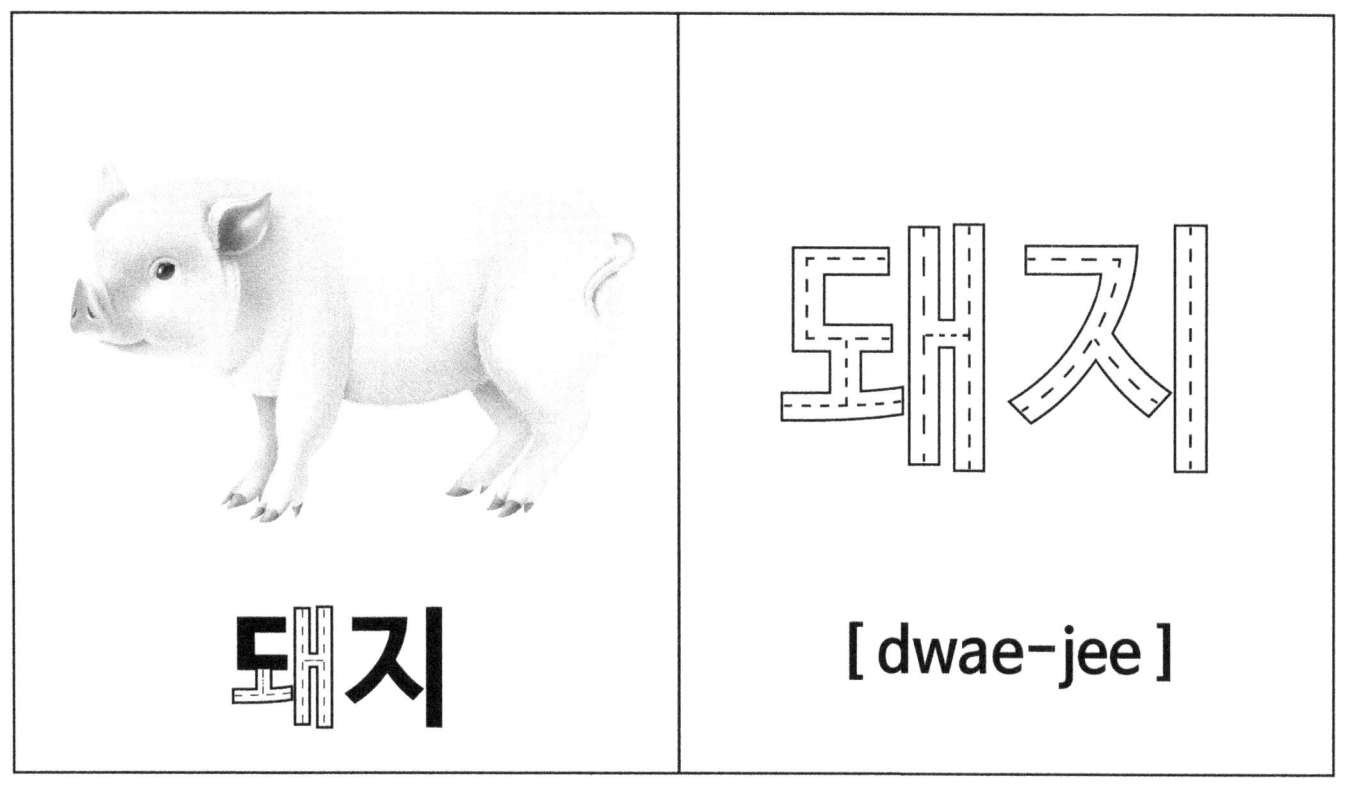

돼지

[dwae-jee]

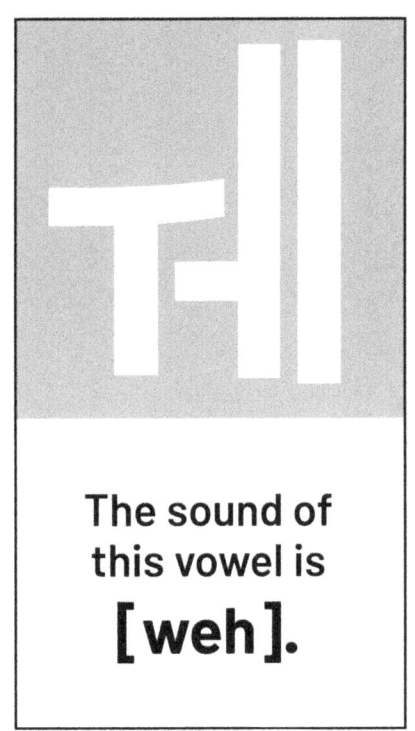

The sound of this vowel is **[weh]**.

ㅞ is for 스웨터
[su-weh-tuh]
sweater

Start on the dot. Trace the dotted line. Use the arrow as a guide.

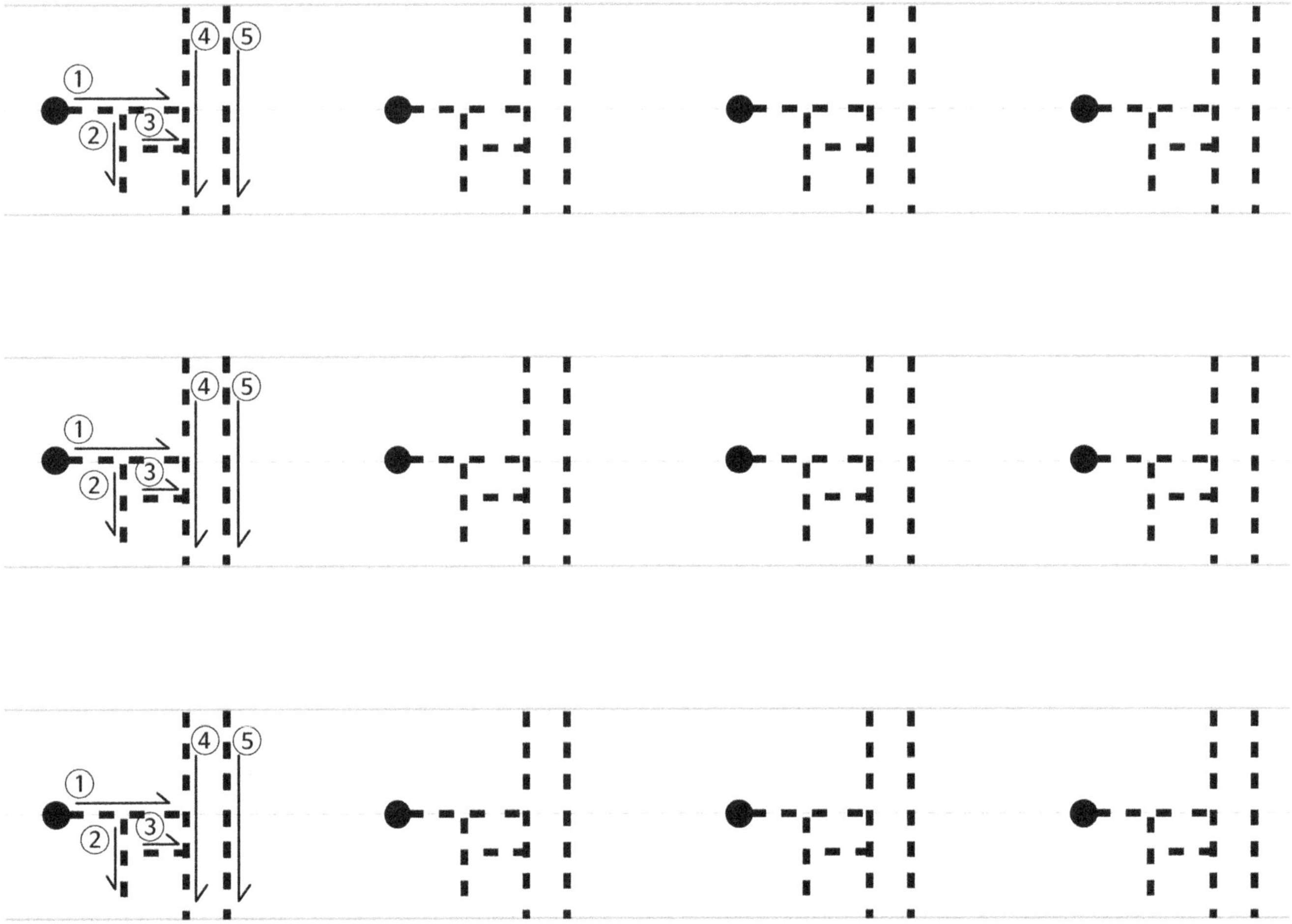

Trace it! Start at the dot! Write it!

웨   웨   웨   웨   웨

Trace the letter. Trace the word.

스웨터

[su-weh-tuh]

UNIT 5

음절
Syllable

Note: In this unit, we learn how to write basic syllables. Syllables are written one letter at a time.

Korean alphabets can be combined like building blocks to create a syllable block. To create a syllable block, you can combine 2 letters (1 consonant + 1 vowel). There are 3 basic ways to do this:

① Side-by-side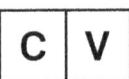

② Top and bottom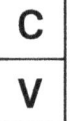

③ Diagonal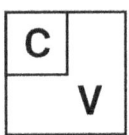

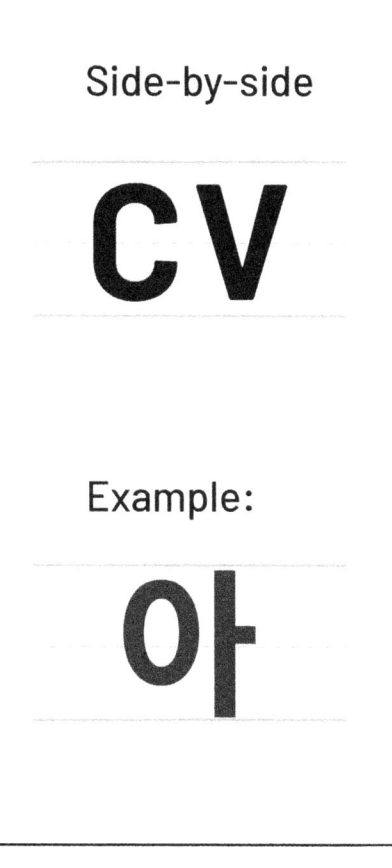

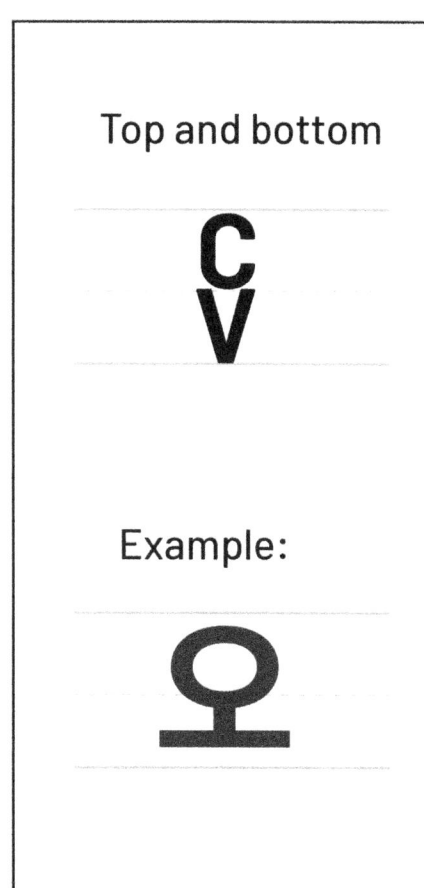

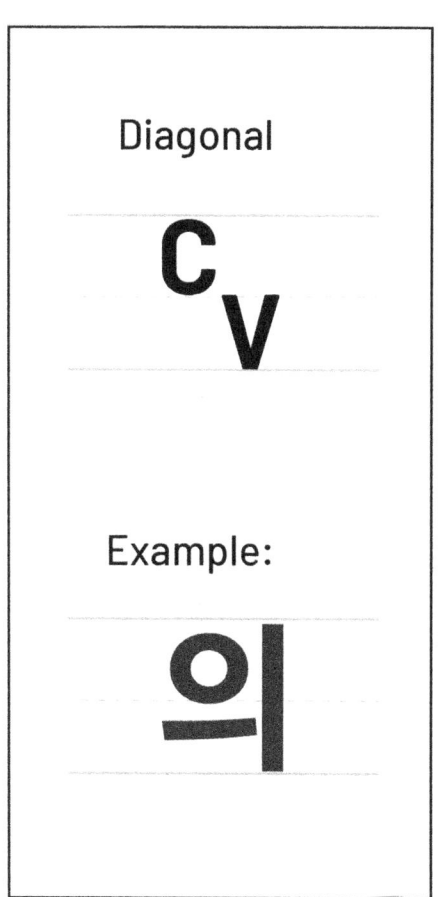

More Examples:

아 야 어 여 이
애 얘 에 예

More Examples:

오 요 우 유 으

More Examples:

의 와 워 위
외 왜 웨

One more thing!
Did you know?
To make a syllable block you can also combine 3 letters (2 consonants + 1 vowel). There are two basic ways to do this:

① Stack them up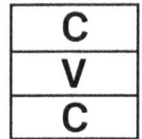

② Side-by-side and bottom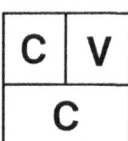

Stack them up	Side-by-side and bottom
C V C	C V C
Example:	Example:
문	책
문 means door.	책 means book.

Other Examples:
- 눈 means eye or snow.
- 곰 means bear.
- 돈 means money.
- 손 means hand.

Other Examples:
- 발 means foot.
- 쌀 means rice.
- 입 means mouth.

Wait! there's more!

Did you know, to create a syllable block, you can even combine 4 letters (3 consonants + 1 vowel).

There are two basic ways to do this:

① Make a square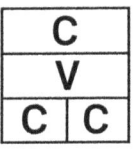

② Make a tower

Make a Square

```
C V
C C
```

Example:

삶 means life.

More Examples:

앉아요 means sit.
읽어요 means read.

Make a tower

```
C
V
C C
```

Example:

흙 means dirt.

More Examples:

긁어요 means scratch.
괜찮아요 means "It's okay."

Practice writing these syllables. Write the consonant first and then the vowel.

가

나

다

라

마

바

사

아

자

차

카

타

파

하

Practice writing these syllables. Write the consonant first and then the vowel.

아

야

어

여

오

요

우

유

으

이

Practice writing these syllables. Write the consonant first and then the vowel.

애

얘

에

예

의

와

워

위

외

왜

웨

CERTIFICATE
OF ACHIEVEMENT

AWARDED TO

for excellence in

LEARN-TO-WRITE KOREAN

Date:

Signed

Author

Eunice Kang, Ph.D. is an educator in Los Angeles, California. Her research areas include South Korea and Korean language policy. Currently, she works at a university as a professor by day and as a writer by night and weekends.

 @eunicekangbooks

Book Designer

Young Jae Koh is a graphic designer based in Los Angeles, California. She has previously worked in Korea and New York as an art director. She loves to watercolor and create art with her daughter.

 @youngjaekoh

CHECK OUT MORE BOOKS BY MIGHTY FORTRESS PRESS!

Made in the USA
Las Vegas, NV
16 January 2022